THE IMPORTANCE OF

John Glenn

These and other titles are included in The Importance Of biography series:

John Glenn

by Rafael Tilton

Lucent Books, P.O. Box 289011, San Diego, CA 92198-9011

Library of Congress Cataloging-in-Publication Data

Tilton, Rafael.
　　John Glenn / by Rafael Tilton.
　　　　p. cm.—(The importance of)
　　Includes bibliographical references and index.
　　　ISBN 1-56006-689-X (alk. paper)
　　　1. Glenn, John, 1921—Juvenile literature. 2. Legislators—
United States—Biography—Juvenile literature. 3. United States.
Congress. Senate—Biography—Juvenile literature. 4.
Astronauts—United States—Biography—Juvenile literature.
[1. Glenn, John, 1921– 2. Legislators. 3. Astronauts.] I. Title.
　　E840.8.G54 T55 2001
　　973.92'092—dc21

　　　　　　　　　　　　　　　　　　　　　　　　　　00-010262

Copyright 2001 by Lucent Books, Inc., P.O. Box 289011,
San Diego, California 92198-9011

Printed in the U.S.A.

Contents

Foreword

THE IMPORTANCE OF biography series deals with individuals who have made a unique contribution to history. The editors of the series have deliberately chosen to cast a wide net and include people from all fields of endeavor. Individuals from politics, music, art, literature, philosophy, science, sports, and religion are all represented. In addition, the editors did not restrict the series to individuals whose accomplishments have helped change the course of history. Of necessity, this criterion would have eliminated many whose contribution was great, though limited. Charles Darwin, for example, was responsible for radically altering the scientific view of the natural history of the world. His achievements continue to impact the study of science today. Others, such as Chief Joseph of the Nez Percé, played a pivotal role in the history of their own people. While Joseph's influence does not extend much beyond the Nez Percé, his nonviolent resistance to white expansion and his continuing role in protecting his tribe and his homeland remain an inspiration to all.

These biographies are more than factual chronicles. Each volume attempts to emphasize an individual's contributions both in his or her own time and for posterity. For example, the voyages of Christopher Columbus opened the way to European colonization of the New World. Unquestionably, his encounter with the New World brought monumental changes to both Europe and the Americas in his day. Today, however, the broader impact of Columbus's voyages is being critically scrutinized. *Christopher Columbus,* as well as every biography in The Importance Of series, includes and evaluates the most recent scholarship available on each subject.

Each author includes a wide variety of primary and secondary source quotations to document and substantiate his or her work. All quotes are footnoted to show readers exactly how and where biographers derive their information, as well as provide stepping stones to further research. These quotations enliven the text by giving readers eyewitness views of the life and times of each individual covered in The Importance Of series.

Finally, each volume is enhanced by photographs, bibliographies, chronologies, and comprehensive indexes. For both the casual reader and the student engaged in research, The Importance Of biographies will be a fascinating adventure into the lives of people who have helped shape humanity's past and present, and who will continue to shape its future.

IMPORTANT DATES IN THE LIFE OF JOHN GLENN

1920 — **1940** — **1950** — **1960** — **1965**

1921
John Glenn is born in Cambridge, Ohio, to John Herschel Glenn Sr. and Clara Sproat Glenn on July 18.

1943
Commissioned in U.S. Marine Corps and assigned to squadron VMO-155 in the South Pacific; marries Annie Castor on April 6.

1959
Glenn joins NASA's Project Mercury on April 6.

1961
Glenn is backup pilot for Alan B. Shepard Jr. on his suborbital flight on May 5; on July 19 Glenn is backup pilot for Virgil A. "Gus" Grissom in the first capsule with a window.

1965
Travels as president of Royal Crown Cola International in January.

1939
Graduates from New Concord High School; enrolls at Muskingum College.

1953
Glenn flies in Korean War as an air force exchange pilot, completing ninety missions; is assigned to the navy's Patuxent River test-pilot school; is assigned to the Bureau of Aeronautics.

1957
As part of Project Bullet, Glenn flies from Los Angeles to New York City in 3 hours and 23 minutes on July 16, breaking the air force speed record.

1962
Glenn, in *Friendship 7*, is the first American to orbit Earth, February 20.

1964
Glenn resigns from NASA on January 17 and starts to campaign for the U.S. Senate; falls and is hospitalized with severe inner ear injury on February 26; in October Glenn is promoted to colonel by President Johnson; retires honorably and without disability from the marines.

1975
Begins first Senate term on January 3.

1978
Principal author of Nuclear Non-Proliferation Act of 1978.

1999
Glenn resigns from Senate on January 3, at end of fourth term; founds the John Glenn Institute.

1981
Glenn begins second Senate term on January 3.

1986
Present when space shuttle *Challenger* explodes in midair on January 28.

1969
Resigns from Royal Crown Cola; announces Senate candidacy.

1970	1975	1980	1985	1990	2000

1970
Defeated in summer primary by Howard Metzenbaum.

1983–1984
Glenn campaigns against Ronald Reagan in presidential race.

1998
On October 29, begins orbital space journey aboard *Discovery* researching aging process.

1987
Begins third Senate term on January 3.

1968
Glenn is present in Los Angeles on June 4 when Robert F. Kennedy is assassinated.

1993
Begins fourth Senate term on January 3.

An American Hero

The achievements of young U.S. Marine John Herschel Glenn Jr. defined the American hero of the twentieth century. His will to succeed, coupled with his initiative, overcame obstacles of physical capacity and educational status, experimental science and untried manufacturing practices, the drama of Cold War competition and the fear of the unknown. And, on February 20, 1962, that will to succeed launched him into space.

Glenn was an achiever from the start. As a grade-school entrepreneur, he sold garden produce to buy a bicycle—the necessary transportation to deliver newspapers. In high school he lettered in three sports. As a World War II pilot, he was known for loyalty to his mission. As a test pilot, he pushed for ever greater limits. As one of the first astronauts, he not only trained for his time in space but also helped improve the design of the spacecraft he eventually used to orbit Earth.

An inveterate self-starter and self-promoter, Glenn was never one to let an issue rest. Once he had made up his mind to fly, he overrode his parents' objections by showing them around the airfield. Once he decided to become a flying ace,

he straddled three branches of the military service to get in his hours and his combat assignments. If an enemy target came within the range of his fighter plane, he stayed in battle until it was destroyed. Continuing his habit of hard work during four terms in the U.S. Senate, he secured a place in U.S. history.

Glenn is a hero who can claim to have defined the space age for two generations of Americans, and throughout his life he has respected those to whom he is a role model. His engaging smile, his unsullied morality, and his faithfulness as a family man and a public figure have not been compromised throughout four decades of name recognition.

In 1998, when he took his interest in the process of aging aboard the space shuttle *Discovery*, he showed that even that frontier from whence no one returns, old age, holds no fear for him. He has been characteristically humble about the possible results of his playing guinea pig above the stratosphere. And *Time* essayist Charles Krauthammer puts into words what many of Glenn's admirers think: "He deserves to go anywhere he wants to go."[1]

A RETROSPECT

In his article "Space Aged," published in the New York Times Magazine, *Thomas Mallon summarizes some of the changes that has taken place between John Glenn's first orbit of Earth and his eight-day flight in the space shuttle* Discovery *nearly thirty-six years later.*

"On February 20, 1962, John Glenn flew over a country with 80 million fewer people than it has today, a land without ZIP codes and throughout which three-quarters of the households still contained both husbands and wives. Most of the wives were home that day, and about the time Friendship 7 was rounding out its third orbit some of the husbands were rounding into a third martini at lunch. The record store down the street from the possibly segregated hotel had yet to stock a Beatles album.

Had the astronaut possessed a more powerful periscope than he did, he still could not have picked out a St. Louis arch or a World Trade Center to serve as a guide post below. Not even Telstar, the early communications satellite, was in the heavens to block his path. The capsule's progress through the skies was relayed by teletype from one tracking station to another. 'In fact,' says Gene Kranz, the legendary controller who was directing the flight that morning, 'probably the most advanced technology we worked with was the Atlantic cable, which had just been relaid in 1956.'

After five hours, Friendship 7, not much bigger than the Stratoloungers [lounge chairs] poised before millions of black-and-white TV sets below, retro-rocketed back to Earth. And as it roared through the atmosphere like 'a real fireball,' in the pilot's own calm words, no one knew for certain that its heat shield wasn't about to fall off.

A young but edgy country, with no idea of the decade it was about to live through, leapt from its chairs and crowed over the man who finally splashed down in the Atlantic. For the next several weeks it heaped gratitude and relief and sheer unjaded delight on the honest-to-God hero—and regular fellow—who had made this wild, necessary ride."

Chapter

1 An All-American Boyhood

John Glenn Jr. was born on July 18, 1921, in Cambridge, Ohio, into a Scottish-Irish family that emphasized the partnership between achievement and religious belief. His father, John Herschel Glenn Sr., usually called Herschel, was the descendant of pioneers who settled on an eighty-acre farm near Claysville, Ohio, before the Civil War. That early generation, as well as the ones that followed, drew their strength and work ethic from attendance at the nearby East Union Presbyterian Church. Surrounded by those strong influences, Herschel Glenn finished six grades of school and then devoted all of his energy to the family farm until he joined the army to serve in World War I.

John's mother, Clara Sproat, met Herschel Glenn at the East Union Presbyterian Church. They married on May 25, 1918, a short time after he entered the army. Clara, a college graduate and schoolteacher, had strong civic and religious values, which translated simply into being a good neighbor and giving wholehearted support to community events. She believed, Glenn later said, that "our relationship to God is a fifty-fifty proposition. God placed us on earth . . .

with certain abilities and talents. How well we use them is completely up to us."[2]

After his military service, Herschel Glenn settled with his wife and infant son in Cambridge. He and a partner, Bertel Welch, started a home-based plumbing business. When young John, who was usually called Bud, was two, the Glenns moved nine miles west to New Concord.

New Concord was at the intersection of the Baltimore and Ohio Railroad and the National Road (later U.S. Route 40), the main road from Baltimore, Maryland, to St. Louis, Missouri. In this middle-class town of about two thousand, Herschel immediately built a house and took in renters. Bud's grandfather and an adopted sister, Jean, soon joined the family. Here, young John Glenn could imagine himself to be, in his words, at "the center of the world."[3]

The Glenns enjoyed life in New Concord. They became a part of the Twice Five Club, a group of five young families who met monthly for potluck dinners. The members of the Twice Five Club and their children became Bud's friends, and one of them, Anna Margaret "Annie" Castor, became his lifelong companion.

New Concord was neighborly and trusting. "Few people locked their doors," remembers Glenn. "If a stranger knocked, you'd let him in and find out what he needed."[4] Basically a religious community centered around the Presbyterian Muskingum College, the town cherished the same strict moral principles with which Herschel and Clara had been raised. Friends, neighbors, and parents encouraged ambition above riches and worldly goods, and they predicted punishment for laziness or laxity in service to God, country, or neighbor. As a result of growing up in this neighborhood, Bud learned to feel great pride in individual achievement.

AN EARLY INTEREST IN AIRPLANES

It was Herschel Glenn who introduced his son to flying. At the age of eight, as Bud rode along on a plumbing job with

John Glenn's parents, John Herschel Glenn Sr. and Clara Glenn, pictured with models of two vehicles that brought their son great fame.

his father, they passed the town airport. It was 1929 and the translatlantic flight of Charles Lindbergh, only two years before, was still a common topic of conversation. So when the pilot of an open-cockpit plane at the airport offered to take the pair up for a spin, both were excited and wanted to go. In his memoir, Glenn writes,

> I probably was scared at the idea of going up, but there wasn't any doubt about it—I wanted to do it. I thought it would be the greatest thing that ever happened. "You mean it?" I said.

> "I sure do," Dad replied. "In fact, if you don't want to do it, I'm going anyway. So you better come unless you want to sit down here and watch."

> We walked over to the plane. It was bigger than I had thought, with two cockpits, one in front of the other. Dad handed the guy some money. He climbed into the backseat, and the pilot helped me up after him. Dad was big, but the seat was wide enough for the two of us, and one strap fit across us both. I could barely see out. The pilot got in front and revved the engine. We bounded down that grass strip and then we were in the air.[5]

A short time later, quarantined during an influenza epidemic, Bud built model airplanes from balsa wood and tissue paper. He hung his collection from his bedroom ceiling and amused himself by imagining what it would be like to fly real airplanes.

A BORN SELF-STARTER

When Bud was eight, the United States found itself caught up in the Great Depression. Working communities like New Concord were some of the first to be affected. A lower standard of living led to a drop in construction, which meant there were few plumbing jobs. So Herschel Glenn joined a Chevrolet dealership in Zanesville, Ohio, and started an additional business selling cars.

The son of a self-made man who was proud of the early success of his plumbing business, young John was not one to ignore the efforts of the hardworking people around him. As hard times deepened and money became scarce, he searched for creative ways to help out his family. He hunted rabbits with his father. In the family garden, he weeded, hoed, harvested, gathered rhubarb, and sold it. "I made some spending money," he writes, "and it wouldn't be long before you could smell rhubarb pie baking all over town."[6]

The rhubarb business was not John's only self-initiated project, though. He seized every opportunity to earn a little money. He washed cars, held a paper route, and put his money in a savings account at the New Concord National Bank.

In 1932 the Glenns came close to losing their home when the bank threatened to foreclose on their mortgage. However, help from President Franklin D. Roosevelt's New Deal came just in time. The New Deal, Roosevelt's plan to revitalize the nation's economy, brought the Works Progress Administration to New Concord to install a town sewer system, and Herschel Glenn's plumbing business gradually improved. Rural Electrification, another New Deal initiative, helped to restore business even more. The Federal Housing Administration renegotiated the Glenns' mortgage and ultimately secured their home ownership, although it did not eliminate poverty from Glenn's childhood memory.

An Upright Upbringing

Herschel and Clara Glenn raised their son, John, with a balanced mixture of discipline, challenge, and good humor. In John Glenn: A Memoir, *Glenn recalls that aspect of his childhood.*

"Some of the older kids went swimming in a pool within Crooked Creek, above our house. I didn't know how to swim yet, and the creek was the one place I was expressly forbidden to go. Regina Regier was an older neighbor girl who took me out to play, possibly out of some maternal instinct. Somehow she got me to go to the creek with her one day. When Mother started calling me and I didn't answer, she came to look for me. She found me at the swimming hole with Regina, and she was mighty unhappy. She ordered me home, then yanked a switch off a bush and followed me. Every time I slowed down, she'd swat my bare legs with that switch. The next day my legs were red with welts. Mother was horrified. She put salve on the welts while I winced, and hugged me, and told me the reason she'd gotten so angry was because she was afraid I had drowned.

That kind of punishment was rare. I didn't do much to anger or upset my parents.

I especially enjoyed being with my father. . . . He could turn very serious at times, and he didn't smoke or drink, but most of the time he was lighthearted. He joked a lot and made me laugh. Part of the fun of being with him was that he was curious. He always wanted to learn about new things, and he would go out of his way to investigate them. Although the Glenn Plumbing Company grew into a successful business of which he was very proud, I think he recognized the limitations of his education. He wanted to give me the curiosity and sense of unbounded possibility that could come from learning."

NOT ALL HARD WORK

Herschel Glenn was not one to let hard times get him down. He belonged to the American Legion, a veterans service organization, and was a loyal attendee at its conventions. Bud sometimes traveled with his father to legion functions, and the young boy was impressed by the closeness of the men who had been in battle together.

He was so impressed that when he was in the fifth grade, Bud started his own organization. Having found an old Boy Scout handbook, he and his friends thought being Scouts would be fun. Since there were no Boy Scout troops in New Concord, the young men formed a club they called the Ohio Rangers. As club president, Bud convinced Reiss Keck, the local fifth-grade teacher, to help them adapt the Boy Scouts' rules and ideals. The self-reliant and enterprising club members made money by providing half-time entertainment at the football games. By the time they entered seventh grade, the Ohio Rangers had built a camp for themselves on a bluff outside of New Concord. As Glenn writes,

> The camp was a second home to me and the other Rangers that summer, 1933. I could hardly wait to finish hoeing and weeding and picking vegetables in our three gardens, and washing cars on the weekends, so I could head for the camp. My friends rushed there, too, when they were finished with their chores. . . . When we were tired of playing we swam in the creek. We cooked hot dogs and hamburgers over our campfire and ate them with baked beans heated in the can, hobo-style. We saluted when we lowered the flag at sunset and I played taps before we went to sleep. We slept in our pup tents, and emerged to a new day the next morning. I usually skipped reveille [the military wake-up trumpet song], but played the colors when we raised the flag. Then we would go home to attack our chores before gathering again in the afternoon. We must have stayed there sixty or seventy days over the course of that summer, and all of us were just in elementary school.[7]

A HIGH-SCHOOL ACHIEVER

New Concord High School, where Bud attended from 1935 to 1939, was another outlet for his enterprising spirit. "Mother and Dad enforced the importance of my role at school," writes Glenn. "They said we all bore responsibilities within the family. Dad's responsibility was to go out and work and make money to support us. Mother's was to keep the home and help him at the store. My job, and Jean's, was to learn and get good grades in school."[8]

John took his role seriously, especially in the sciences and in civics. Not only did he get good grades, but he also spent after-school hours with Julian White, a chemistry major at Muskingum College, expanding his science background. He learned the workings of a radio, and his imagination was ignited by a dynamic course on the in-

John Glenn took school seriously and participated in extracurricular activities. Here he is pictured (seated, second from left) with his fellow high school newspaper staff members.

stitutions of government and politics. During the evening meal, he and his family reported on their day's work, sharing and discussing their experiences.

John rounded out his high-school years by participating in extracurricular activities. He served on the student council, worked as a reporter for the New Concord High School paper the *Maroon and White Newslite*, and played trumpet with the town's marching band. On the school's football, basketball, and tennis teams, according to a teammate, "[Glenn] wasn't what you would call a great athlete, but he sure was a fine team player."[9]

John also served as president of the junior class and convinced his classmates that their junior-senior banquet/prom theme should draw a parallel between flying and the future. "We were, after all," writes Glenn in his memoir, "a class of juniors about to soar into seniorhood, and the seniors were flying off to college, jobs, or marriage. My schoolmates approved the theme; we put a picture of a Ford Trimotor airplane on the program cover, and I and my senior counterpart, as toastmasters of the event, were designated as the evening's 'pilots.'"[10]

On weekends John indulged other interests. Helping Herschel Glenn with the Chevrolet dealership, John learned enough mechanics to fix second-hand cars. He also moved the cars to different spots around the lot and passed his driver's test when he was fifteen.

He loved to travel, and with his former Ohio Rangers counselor, Reiss Keck, he shared a driving tour to Montreal, Niagara Falls, Valley Forge, New York, and Philadelphia. The travelers toured a steel mill and an electric power plant. These visits taught him, he said, along with the understanding of hydraulics and generators and steel manufacture, the value of active curiosity. "Idle curiosity," he concluded, "was the same as daydreaming; it didn't get you one step closer to what you wanted to know."[11]

EARLY CHOICES

Throughout his school years, John maintained a relationship with Annie Castor. A year older than he, she had been his playmate since he was two. At first she was a friend who prevailed on him to convince his fellow Rangers to lend their camp to the girls. Then she became a regular at local ice cream socials, cookouts, and swimming and skating parties. Finally, they paired off as a couple. Of that time, Glenn recalls in his memoir, "I had always liked Annie's smile. It revealed all the warmth and eagerness that was there, though hidden to some by the difficulty she had speaking. Now her smile struck me in a different way. It was like a pleasant trap that held me so I couldn't look away. I started to look forward to that feeling."[12]

Theirs was a relationship that reflected thoughtfulness and respect. Annie had a pronounced and persistent stutter, for which some classmates teased her. John, however, never made her feel self-conscious about her stuttering and confronted anyone he heard making fun of her. Her speech, says Glenn, "wasn't something I viewed as a problem. Her father stuttered, too, though not as severely. It was just something she did, no different from some people writing left-handed and others right-handed."[13]

John and Annie saw each other regularly, as both belonged to the school orchestra and the town marching band. An accomplished musician, Annie played piano and organ. In the marching band she played trombone, and John played the trumpet.

As she neared the end of her senior year, the couple began to talk of marriage and even considered going to Kentucky, where teenagers could buy a marriage license. It was a trip they ultimately decided not to make, however. As he faced his senior year, John realized that neither he nor Annie was ready for the level of commitment marriage demanded.

CAREER AND COLLEGE PLANS

As the summer before his senior year ended, John again began to dream of flying. He and a cousin, Robert Thompson, joined their fathers on a trip to Cleveland for the National Air Races. They stayed only one of the three days of the races, but daredevil pylon races, aerobatic stunt flying, and parachute jumping were attention-riveting events. Recalling the Thompson Trophy race, in which planes flew thirty laps at high speed around a ten-mile oval course, Glenn writes, "The pilots banked tight

---

AVIATION IN OHIO

In his National Geographic *article entitled "John Glenn: Man with a Mission," William R. Newcott describes John Glenn's hometown of New Concord, Ohio.*

"From the time he was born in 1921, John Glenn saw people going places. His childhood home, in New Concord, stood on a hill overlooking the National Road, the first federal highway and one of the pioneers' earliest routes west.

'When they widened the road, we had to move the house up the hill,' [Glenn] said. It's there, still, unmarked, right near the new John Glenn High School, where on fall weekends the John Glenn Muskies football team fights for old JG.

A walk down Main Street tells the story of Glenn's life. There's the old high school building where he attended classes with Annie, his childhood sweetheart. And the long drive that leads to Muskingum College, where they both earned degrees. If you head down to the veterans' park and look at the big brass plaque that commemorates local boys who marched off to World War II, there—between Raymond M. Glass and Leonard A. Goff—you'll find John H. Glenn, Jr. (Just above, in the list of World War I vets, is John H. Glenn, Sr.)

Stop into the coffee shop, and along with your menu you can pick up vintage laminated pages from the Zanesville *Times Recorder* tracing the favorite son's career. Seems he was a local hero long before anyone dreamed of sealing him into a space capsule."

---

around high pylons and thundered right past the spectators. I loved the roar of those engines and the sheer speed of the planes, and when it was over, . . . flying beckoned me as never before."[14]

Soon, however, John became immersed in his senior year and had no time for airplanes. Once again flying took a back seat to other activities. He played on his school's championship football and basketball teams. He became sports editor of the paper and took a part in the senior class play. By his graduation in the spring of 1939, he was committed to a job as a YMCA summer camp counselor and a trip with his family to the New York World's Fair.

Marriage with Annie Castor, meanwhile, became a "when," not an "if," as he planned to enter Muskingum College, where she was already enrolled. That fall he made an easy transition into the small college, where courses were geared toward the humanities and the teaching of character. Glenn settled in and became a chemistry major.

Family finances dictated that Glenn hold a job and live at home rather than on campus, saving the cost of room and board. He applied for a work scholarship and soon settled into a routine of classes, student council, football, and basketball.

Following his freshmen year and another summer at the YMCA camp, Glenn had two things on his mind. The first had to do with rumors that the United States might draft young men his age into the war in Europe. The second issue was with his chemistry major, where mathematics

was becoming a serious problem. As Glenn later explained, "Organic chemistry required a level of mathematics that I had not yet taken. I had either jumped in over my head, or the college had let me take a course it shouldn't have. I was passing, but I was struggling, and I was going to have to refocus my major very soon."[15]

A NEW COLLEGE ROUTINE

After Christmas vacation of his sophomore year, refocusing his major not only looked possible but desirable as well. The physics department was recruiting applicants for the Civilian Pilot Training Program. The opportunity to fly was all Glenn needed to become a physics major. Even when his parents expressed disappointment with his new decision—they felt the dangers of flying outweighed the career potential—Glenn was determined and continued with his plans.

He and four other Muskingum men from the physics department passed the physical exam and were accepted into the pilot training course. By April 1941 they had completed their preliminary classroom courses and traveled sixty miles to New Philadelphia, Ohio, to see the airfield where they would take actual flight training.

The program used as its training aircraft a Taylor, which flew at around ninety miles per hour. The intensive course included taxis, level flight, medium turns, taking off, climbing, gliding, landing, S turns, and figure eights. As Glenn recalls,

John Glenn and his wife Annie in 1965.

The plane soon felt natural in my hands, and the increasingly complicated maneuvers . . . also seemed to come naturally to me. The total attention that flying demanded was exhilarating. I felt when I was in the air that all my senses were operating at their fullest. I enjoyed the challenge of learning just what I could do, and the more I did, the more I realized I could do. I thought that flying was a skill at which I might, in time, learn to excel.[16]

Flight training progressed rapidly. Each student flew solo in May. Then, "after just two weeks of solo practice," writes Glenn, "we moved on to precision maneuvers. . . . At the end of the first week of June, we made our cross-country solo flights [and]

crammed on the Civil Pilot Training Manual for our examination."[17]

THE PEARL HARBOR ATTACK

The cramming paid off, and although not quite twenty-one, Glenn received his pilot's license. He returned to college that fall, and, in addition to working hard on mathematics and serving on the football team, he tried to save money for some flying time.

It was 1941, though, and news of the war in Europe was everywhere. In early December, when John was on his way to Annie's senior organ recital he heard over the radio that the Japanese had attacked Pearl Harbor. After her performance they talked, and John made a decision: "I have to go,"[18] he told her.

GLENN'S FATHER AS AN AIRPLANE PASSENGER

John Glenn's memories include many that involve flying. This one, recounted in his John Glenn: A Memoir, *details the near disaster of the first time he took his father up in an airplane.*

"One day I told Dad I wanted to take him up.

We drove to the airfield in Zanesville on a day toward the end of the summer, and I rented a small plane for an hour. Dad climbed in while I did the preflight run-through, checking fuel and oil levels and the condition of the plane. When he got in, the plane sagged. Dad was heavy then. He probably weighed 230 pounds, not loose fat but a thickness of muscle from hard work and a healthy appetite for Mother's cooking. I weighed 175, and his arms were almost as big as my legs. I got in, taxied to a corner of the field, and turned for takeoff.

It was a hot day, indicating less dense air, which provides less engine power and less wing lift. But things seemed all right as I started down the field. We went through a dip in the grass runway, and a row of trees at the far end started getting closer. I had the throttle wide open. The engine strained, but we weren't developing the expected speed for takeoff. The trees kept getting closer. I was afraid to look at Dad, and didn't have time to do it, anyway. I saw those trees coming toward me, and I began to have some doubt about whether we were going to get off the ground. We just barely had takeoff speed when we came to the far end of the field with the trees still ahead of us. I pulled back on the stick and the plane struggled up over the trees and dipped down again, following the land behind them that sloped down to the Muskingum River. With the engine running wide open we gradually got enough speed to finally start climbing.

When I had the nerve to look at Dad, he was unclenching his grip on the edge of the seat. But his eyes were twinkling behind his horn-rimmed glasses and he said, 'Like those exciting takeoffs, do you?'"

Glenn quit college and signed up for the U.S. Army Air Corps. As he writes,

> I was sold on flying as soon as I had a taste of it. As a matter of fact, I think I would have tried to get into some branch of flying along about this time even if the war had not come along. My friends and I each had approximately 65 hours of flying time in the course. We were solo for about 30 of these hours. I was one of the first in the group to go up alone.[19]

With his basic flight training behind him, Glenn thought that signing up and being sworn in for the army would take him to the front lines. When orders still had not come by March 1942, however, he and his friends decided to join the navy. They went to the navy recruiter, took the exam, passed, and were sworn in. "It's just possible that I've been AWOL [absent without leave] from the Army ever since,"[20] Glenn later quipped.

Navy orders came quickly, but before Glenn left for training in Olathe, Kansas, he asked Annie to marry him. She accepted and they said good-bye at the New Concord train station. Glenn writes,

> Annie and I had seen each other almost every day for nearly twenty years. For the last six or seven of those years we had been learning that love is a combination of passion, friendship, and respect. I hated to leave her, not really knowing what lay ahead except the opportunity and obligation to serve my country in a time of need. We kissed for a long time before the conductor called, "All aboard." I was still touching her hand when the train started moving.[21]

2 A Soldier in Two Wars

Navy flight training started with physical education, competitive sports, and tests of endurance. Classroom instruction in naval regulations, navigation, engines, and the spotting of enemy aircraft preceded the actual flying lessons. For John Glenn, those were not the only activities. Every day also included time for writing a letter to Annie, who had graduated from Muskingum College in May and had taken a job as a secretary for the U.S. Army Air Corps in Dayton, Ohio.

The navy planes, which were bigger and faster than the aircraft that Glenn had trained in, required both flight time and classroom instruction. However, Glenn quickly became accustomed to them. He said, "I began to develop . . . the kinesthetics of flying—a feeling that the plane was an extension of myself. My hands moved on the controls without my having to think about it, and the plane responded to my thought."[22]

From Olathe, Kansas, Glenn moved to the Naval Air Training Center at Corpus Christi, Texas, and started a new level of training that emphasized instrument flying, weapons, and tactics. Mathematics continued to be a challenge for Glenn, but

a friend, Tom Miller from George West, Texas, tutored him on the subject. Together they listened to the war news and worked hard to bring their flying skills up to the high standards demanded by the navy.

Impatient to get into action, Glenn began to think of taking advantage of a privilege naval pilots had at his stage of training. He could apply to transfer his commission (rank as an officer) to the U.S. Marine Corps. When both Glenn and Miller graduated in the top 10 percent of their class, they applied for the marines, hoping they could fly the newest, fastest fighter, the Lockheed P-38 Lightning. The plane boasted a cruise speed of 290 miles per hour and carried an arsenal of machine guns and cannon. As they waited and hoped for their assignments, they got valuable experience in gunnery and bombing and even some actual patrolling in the Gulf of Mexico, where some enemy U-boats had been sighted.

His cadet training complete and his wings earned, Glenn was commissioned second lieutenant, U.S. Marine Corps, on March 31, 1943. He then took his fifteen-day leave to marry Annie. Their wedding took place in New Concord on April 6, 1943, at the Presbyterian Church that both the Glenns and the Castors attended. After a brief honeymoon at a hotel in Columbus, Ohio, the newlyweds drove their wedding present, a black 1934 Chevrolet from the Glenn car lot, to the Marine Corps Air Station in Cherry Point, North Carolina.

Of his time in North Carolina, Glenn writes,

> Training filled every day. We spent mornings in classes on weapons, engines, navigation, combat tactics, and Marine history, worked in special trainers designed for aircraft recognition, and sat in black-out rooms for night-vision training. In the afternoons [the program's supervisor] sent us running in the steamy North Carolina lowlands. But the one thing we didn't train in was flying. Because of a shortage of aircraft, we had trouble even getting the four hours a month required to earn flight pay.[23]

Glenn and Annie found a small apartment about twenty miles from the base, but they were in North Carolina for only three weeks when the marines relocated Glenn's squadron to California, where there was more chance of flight training. The couple bought a 1939 Chevrolet on credit and drove west to the Naval Auxiliary Air Station at Kearny Mesa, near San Diego.

ANOTHER TRANSFER

Getting into the actual war was still not all that easy. The Kearny Mesa base was training transport pilots, not fighters. But

The Lockheed P-38 Lightning was a plane Glenn wanted to fly during the war.

A Preview of Fighter Piloting

Biographer Frank Van Riper, in Glenn: The Astronaut Who Would Be President, *recounts the visit Charles A. Lindbergh made to El Centro, California, where the young John Glenn was learning to fly F-4F Wildcats and Corsair fighter planes.*

"At El Centro, Glenn would have a glimpse of his future in the person of Charles Lindbergh, to whom he would be compared after his orbital flight in space. In 1943, Glenn, an anonymous young pilot, actually met the world-famous aviator when he made a brief stop at the air station. The 'Lone Eagle,' who had conquered the Atlantic in the *Spirit of St. Louis* some 16 years earlier, was serving the military as an advisor and had also accompanied American pilots on combat missions in the Pacific.

One afternoon in the fall of '43, Lindbergh flew into El Centro in one of the new versions of the Corsair, without the 'birdcage' dome. Glenn stood gape-mouthed as he stared at the plane and its legendary pilot. Glenn and [his friend Tom] Miller walked out to meet the plane. As they approached Lindbergh, the Marine major he was talking to introduced the brash young fliers. Glenn immediately told Lindbergh how much he had admired him from the time he could first read. Glenn's boyhood bedroom at New Concord, filled with balsa wood airplane models, contained numerous books about Lindbergh's solo flight across the Atlantic in 1927. For all the deferential admiration, however, Glenn was not content to shake hands and gawk.

'Colonel Lindbergh,' Glenn asked, 'is there any chance of us getting to fly that plane?'

To their surprise, Lindbergh grinned his agreement. 'Sure, I'd be glad to let you fly her,' he said. Today, Glenn remembers Lindbergh as a 'quiet individual who gave us a lot of information about the new specifications of the Corsair.' He adds that Lindbergh, who lived to see Glenn's space flight in 1962, wired his congratulations, repaying over a span of 35 years the admiration Glenn felt for the first man to fly solo across the Atlantic."

Glenn and Tom Miller, who had also been relocated to California, had fighter planes on their minds. And the two were becoming adept at working their way through the system to achieve what they wanted. Following a hunch, Glenn and Miller asked if they could join the heavier-than-air-marine-observation (VMO) fighter squadron. They were encouraged by Major John P. Haines Jr., to go through the proper channels for a transfer.

More impatient than ever, Glenn (but not Miller) made the mistake of thinking he could shortcut the approval process. It was his immediate officer, Major Zoney, who realized, when the transfers came through, that Glenn had gone above his head. Zoney told Glenn that he would never get a flying commission. "What you did was insubordination and I won't tolerate it,"[24] Zoney said, and he included Miller in the threat.

Glenn, however, was not ready to give up and accept the fact that he had ruined his chances as well as Miller's. "I apologized profusely and did everything I could to smooth things over," Glenn later explained. "Zoney finally relented and gave me his permission to reapproach Colonel Roberts [the superior officer]. I made my pitch, but I didn't have high hopes."[25]

The commission to the fighter squadron came through, and Glenn and Miller were assigned to the Imperial Valley, located northeast of San Diego near the Salton Sea. Their training included practice bombing and competitive scorekeeping, first in Wildcat fighter planes and then in the newer Corsairs.

Glenn was one of the first lieutenants to flight-test an improved model of the Corsair. As he recalls,

> After a half hour in the new Corsair, I loved it that much more. The cockpit was raised a little, and [in comparison with the older ones] you could see much better out of the bubble canopy. Landing was a lot less touchy [than in the old Corsairs]. You still couldn't see ahead while you were taxiing, but that was a small thing. Corsair pilots were used to zigzagging when they taxied, looking out one side of the plane and then the other. A whole squadron taxiing looked like some kind of a primitive dance performed by crabs scuttling in formation.[26]

AN OVERSEAS ASSIGNMENT

Glenn's next move would be overseas. On February 5, 1944, he left first for Hawaii and then continued on to Midway Island.

As a fighter pilot based on Midway Island, Glenn's job was to attack Japan's supply routes and navy ships. During his four-month duty as a member of the VMO-155 squadron under John P. Haines Jr., Glenn proved his dependability and toughness flying the Corsairs he loved. His squadron's target-hit averages were 6 to 7 percent better than any other group's.

After nearly three months Glenn's squadron was relieved, and he was relocated to the Marshall Islands. In one set of seven consecutive patrol flights over the

Marshall Islands, Glenn logged more hours than any of the other thirty-seven pilots on the roster.

INTO COMBAT

Glenn's first combat mission took place while he was in the Marshall Islands on August 10, 1944. It was the first time that he had come under fire, and it was also the first time that he had lost a squadron mate, Lieutenant Miles "Monty" Goodman. In his memoir, Glenn talks about the air battle of August 10:

> I hit several targets as I came across the island from the south. Streams of tracer fire came at us from the ground. I pulled out very low on the treetops, banked to the east, and climbed to the rendezvous point. As far as I could tell, I had not been hit.

Looking back at the island, I saw a series of explosions. . . . Up high, black puffs of smoke hung in the air from the large-caliber antiaircraft fire directed at [our] bombers.

We had to go to eight thousand feet to find a clear spot in the clouds to rendezvous. I heard one of the dive-bomber pilots say on the radio that he had seen a plane go down. Seven of us joined up at the rendezvous. Monty was missing.[27]

Glenn was deeply affected by the death of his wingman and good friend. "I had never felt so helpless," he writes in his memoir. "I stood there and sobbed."[28] Glenn wrote a personal letter to Goodman's family in Harrisburg, Pennsylvania, praising his friend's skill as a pilot and his faithfulness to his comrades in action.

Despite the loss, the men's practice and training with F-4U Corsairs continued.

An F-4U Corsair fighter pilot releases rocket projectiles. The Corsair was the plane Glenn flew in combat during World War II.

Glenn's squadron, often led by Glenn himself, experimented with ways to improve weapons and technique. Their revolutionary tactics involved using their landing gear to slow them down so bombs could be dropped more accurately. In his memoir, Glenn explains:

> The dive bombers had dive brakes. These were large, sometimes split flaps that came out into the airstream to slow the dive. With the Corsair, we had a different kind of dive brake. Our technique was to come down from high above a target and drop the landing gear. The gear and their flat plate fairings acted as an air brake, making a bombing run slower, more stable, and more accurate. Our bomb runs hit a higher percentage of their targets than they would if we had come in at full speed. You would drop your bomb load, pull out and raise the gear, then jink [dodge] away in a series of quick maneuvers that made it hard for the antiaircraft gunners [on the ground] to hold an aim point ahead of you that would get a hit.[29]

STARTING A FAMILY AS A CAREER MARINE

In February 1945 Glenn returned to the United States for his year of home duty. After being assigned to the U.S. Marine Corps Air Station at Cherry Point, North Carolina, he took leave in New Concord, Ohio, and was reunited with Annie.

One of the first adjustments and decisions the couple made was to start their family. Together again, they moved into a hotel on Maryland's Chesapeake Bay, a few miles from the Naval Air Test Center on the Patuxent River. From there, Glenn could commute to the base for his new duties, which included accelerated service tests on new planes.

Promoted to the rank of captain in July, and still on home duty at the end of the war in August, Glenn was also faced with the decision of whether to make a career of the U.S. Marines. Since his enlistment was ending and Annie was pregnant, both his father and his father-in-law had begun to plan for his return to civilian life. His father wanted him to come back to the family business, but his father-in-law counseled him to take up dentistry. Glenn put them both off, wanting to continue flying, wondering if civilian airlines would be to his liking, waiting to see if he would be promoted, and realizing that the war had changed him more than anyone had realized.

When the promotion with its higher salary did come through, Glenn knew he could support his family and do what he wanted. Recalling those days in his memoir, he writes,

> I liked the Marine Corps, I liked the life, and I particularly liked that kind of flying. Annie and I talked it over. I think in the back of her mind she had never really expected we would settle down in New Concord after the war. She knew how much I loved flying, not just from me but from pilots I had served with. She had learned what I would never tell her in so many words—that I was proud of my ability

THE BIRTH OF JOHN DAVID GLENN

John Glenn's A Memoir *is filled with poignant references to his wife, Annie, and their children, such as this one about the birth of their son, John David.*

"I helped Annie into the car in the pouring rain, and we started down the road to Camp Lejeune.

The wipers in the Chevy were the one thing I hadn't thought to check. The rain was blinding. Every minute or so we'd be rattled by a thunderclap. Every jagged flash of lightning showed an expanse of rainsoaked swampy countryside with no houses and no lights. Annie's pains kept getting closer together, the rain kept pouring down, and I tried to remember what little I knew about being a midwife. The cries 'Towels! Hot water!' came to me from half-remembered movies, but the only hot water was in the radiator and we had no towels, only a bundle of baby blankets.

We finally got to the hospital at about four-thirty in the morning. Annie delivered our son, John David, only two hours later. He weighed seven pounds thirteen ounces, and had Annie's dark hair and a strong, insistent voice. He was beautiful, and we loved him from the moment we saw him."

as a pilot. Part of my love for her grew from knowing that she understood me so perfectly. She knew that flying had become part of who I was, and she was proud of me.[30]

BACK OVERSEAS

Three months after their son, John David "Dave," was born on December 13, 1945, Glenn was transferred to El Toro, south of Los Angeles, California. There, he refined his flying skills in air shows that demonstrated for civilians the capabilities of Corsairs. He also became a qualified mechanic, doing his own tune-ups and maintenance, a result of the base's peacetime budget cutbacks.

As the young family began to settle in, enjoying the beaches and the mountains, it seemed that Glenn's life as a career marine was ideal. Soon, however, Annie discovered she was pregnant with their second child, and Glenn realized that his year of home duty was up; he was due for another overseas assignment. He had heard rumors that short tours of three to six months could be served in China, and thinking he would be back before the baby was born, he asked for and obtained an assignment to Nan Yuan Field, south of Beijing, China.

In China, beginning in December 1946, Glenn logged seventy-five hours of flight time in jets while serving on patrol with marine fighter squadron VMF-218. The squadron flew surveillance missions, air-dropped food to starving people, and, in their visits to the markets near their headquarters, learned a little about the poverty that had spawned Chinese interest in Communism. As Glenn recalls,

> Evidence of poverty was everywhere. The rickshaw [small hand-drawn carts used as taxis] drivers ate rice with weak soup they bought from vendors, who boiled the soup from animal entrails in large barrels on the street corners. Many of them slept next to or in their rickshaws, pulled up under the eaves of buildings. . . .
>
> We were there to support the peace teams and encourage peace, but even as much against Communism as I was, I couldn't help but wonder why the Chinese people hadn't revolted sooner. I didn't see that they had a whole lot to lose.[31]

When Glenn's three months in China were up, his commanding officer informed him that his overseas tour had been extended. Instead of heading home, Glenn would be sent to the Pacific island of Okinawa, one of the navy's fueling stations, and then on to the Naval Air Station on the island of Guam.

FIFTEEN MONTHS ON OKINAWA

On March 15, 1947, before Glenn was even settled on Okinawa, Annie gave birth to a daughter, Carolyn Ann "Lyn," in a hospital near Zanesville, Ohio. "It hurt not to be there," Glenn reflected later. "I hadn't envisioned our life being like that, but I was buoyed by the news that they both were doing fine, and I passed out cigars."[32]

A week later, however, another message came—Annie had contracted a life-threatening infection. Glenn headed home immediately, not knowing if Annie would be there to greet him. It took five days to reach the United States, but when he did, he found Annie recovering well. Relieved, Glenn spent his two days off with her and their son and infant daughter.

Upon returning to the Pacific, Glenn found that his squadron had moved to the Naval Air Station on Guam. There he spent most of his time building Quonset huts (half-cylinder metal structures) for the navy families stationed on the island. Finally, after a year, he obtained permission to bring Annie and the two children to Guam. They lived there for three months, able to take time to explore the island and enjoy the beach together when Glenn was not on duty.

In 1947, Glenn moved to the naval air station on Guam, an assignment that resulted in his staying on the island for more than a year.

A FLIGHT INSTRUCTOR IN TEXAS AND ARIZONA

Glenn's assignment on Guam ended in December 1948, when he was sent back to the Naval Air Training Center at Corpus Christi, Texas. For the first three months, while he waited to start his actual assignment, instructor of pilots, he worked on shore patrol. He supervised a staff of four military police and a navy medic, something totally new to him and rather mundane. "Most of the calls we got," Glenn writes in his memoir, "had to do with

drinking, fistfights, or a combination of the two."[33]

When his shore patrol assignment was up, he took a six-week training course at the Instructors Advanced Training Unit in preparation for his flight instructor duties. While there, he compared the marine courses with those in the navy and air force and saw where improvements could be made. Subsequently, his commanding officers incorporated his suggestions into the program and extended his training to include a three-month course at Williams Air Force Base in Arizona.

GLENN IS HIT BY ANTIAIRCRAFT FIRE

In his article "A Past to Draw On," for the anthology We Seven, *by the Astronauts Themselves, John Glenn gives this vignette of one of his narrow escapes in his fighter-pilot days.*

"One day over Korea, for example, I got hit by antiaircraft fire just as I was starting on an enemy target with a load of napalm. At an altitude of 8,000 feet, as I was rolling in to make the attack, I heard and felt a big bang outside the plane, and it rolled sharply to the left. The pilot behind me radioed that he saw a big ball of smoke and that I had been hit. I still had control and turned immediately towards the sea, about 30 miles away, figuring that if I had to ditch I would rather wind up in the water, which our Navy pretty well controlled, rather than in Communist territory. The enemy shell had knocked out part of my trim controls, along with a three-foot section of the right wing. I was able to get up to about 15,000 feet, where I slowed to landing speed and determined that I could still control the airplane in that condition. I headed for our base near Pohang [in central eastern South Korea], and made it home with no further difficulty. After I landed, we saw that the shell—which was about the equivalent of our own 90-millimeter antiaircraft—had hit the napalm tank first, under the wing. This had partially cushioned the explosion and saved the airplane from being torn apart. Though we found pieces of shrapnel as big as a man's thumb inside the fuel tank, the tank had sealed itself up around the holes and had left me enough fuel to get home."

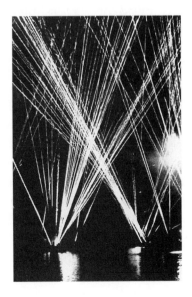

Antiaircraft fire streams into the air. John Glenn experienced close encounters with such fire during his military service.

At Williams, Glenn was introduced to and flew his first jets. "I [soon] learned," he wrote later, "that jets changed everything. I'd been used to doing things at three hundred miles per hour, and now suddenly I was doing them at six hundred miles per hour. . . . But I got used to the new feel of jets quickly."[34]

THE KOREAN WAR

Glenn's skill with jets was all too soon in demand. On June 25, 1950, in a surprise attack, North Korea invaded South Korea. The ensuing Korean War, fought by United Nations (UN) forces that included troops from the United States, Great Britain, and other Western nations, began five days later.

The hostilities made Glenn's work as flight instructor all the more important. He continued at Corpus Christi until June 1951. With the possibility of more overseas duty ahead, he was assigned first to Quantico, Virginia, for the marines' six-month Amphibious Warfare School, and then he was assigned to his old base, Cherry Point, North Carolina, for a jet refresher course. On February 9, 1953, as soon as his refresher course was over, John Glenn applied for combat duty. As a member of marine fighter squadron VMF-311, he flew Panther jets on bomber missions during the Korean War.

AN EXCHANGE PILOT WITH THE AIR FORCE

Always eager to fly, Glenn took advantage of another program that allowed pilots to transfer from marine duty into UN patrol duty with the air force. As an air force exchange pilot, he flew Sabre jets along the Yalu River, which formed the North Korea–China border. Chinese sympathizers often made raids into UN territory, and Glenn hoped for the chance to attack some of the enemy's Russian-made MiGs—fast fighters similar to the Sabre in looks and maneuverability.

For more than three months, combat with the MiGs remained a faraway goal. Finally, between July 12 and 22, Glenn got his chance. He shot down three MiGs.

On July 27, 1953, the Korean War ended. Glenn's fellow marine and biographer Lieutenant Colonel Philip N. Pierce, notes that Glenn's last air-to-air combat made history. His squadron flew "the only mission during the entire war where a four-plane Sabre flight scored three confirmed kills."[35]

In two wars, Glenn received the Distinguished Flying Cross and six Air Medals. He had flown a total of 149 missions, 59 in the Corsair (propeller plane), 63 in the Panther jet, and 27 in the Sabre jet. But in the end, he was ready to go home.

3 Test Pilot

Glenn found that his Korean War experience and the excitement of flying in combat made most peacetime military jobs unappealing to him. One job, however, testing the efficiency of new planes, sounded like a chance to continue flying as well as to use his ability to react quickly in difficult situations. He could also become a higher paid and higher ranking officer.

Biographer Peter N. Carroll considers Glenn's application to the testing center at Patuxent, Maryland, an attempt "to prolong the sense of adventure by volunteering as a military test pilot."[36] Before he could apply for this prized position, though, he had to obtain a number of endorsements from his former officers. He put pressure on his superiors—in particular, his air force exchange commanding officer, Colonel John L. Smith—to open the door to what he wanted.

The job at Patuxent, Glenn realized, also required more education than his two years at Muskingum College. "I had decided I wanted to get into test work," Glenn told interviewers. "But test pilot training involves a lot of math and calculus, which I didn't have."[37] With determination, and against terrific odds, Glenn set out to overcome his deficiencies. To pass

calculus in a class designed by the University of Maryland as a brushup, he had to start from scratch with primary textbooks, which he plowed through in the midnight hours. One of his classmates, Tom Miller, recalls, "Boy, did he study. He left Annie back in Ohio during those early days and just kept his nose in his books."[38]

Glenn was assigned to the Patuxent River Naval Air Station in rural southern Maryland. He reported to the base at the end of January 1954 and passed the eight-month marine test-pilot school in August. While Annie and the family looked on, he received his assignment as project officer on several new airplanes, including the Chance Vought F-8U Crusader, which was supposed to fly faster than sound travels. John Glenn was thirty-three years old, too old for active service, but focused on advancing both his military career and the image of the U.S. Marine Corps.

THE DAILY WORK OF A TEST PILOT

Life as a pilot on the Patuxent base was fulfilling for a man who had his heart set on flying. His job was to test the design of

At the age of thirty-three, Glenn took a job as a test pilot, a move which allowed him to advance his military career.

new planes and armaments. In his memoir, Glenn describes the process of finding out just how well the equipment worked:

> Testing in each area began with the so-called design envelope—the chart of speed, altitude, Gs [the pressure one feels as a result of acceleration], loading, and weapons-system performance that the designers believed the plane capable of. "Filling out the envelope" meant systematically doing flight after flight under different conditions to fill in blank spots on the charts—the envelope—in each test area to determine what the plane would actually do safely. You started at the lower left with points in the minimum-performance range and gradually worked points to the right

and up, out to the design limits. When you reached the upper right corner of the chart you were "pushing the envelope."[39]

GLENN CONCEIVES OF AND PROMOTES PROJECT BULLET

For two years Glenn was a top test pilot at the Patuxent base. When his assignment ended, he was transferred to a desk job at the Bureau of Aeronautics in Washington, D.C. The new office job made him restless, so Glenn began looking for a ticket out of the bureaucracy. Ultimately, it was his experience in testing the Chance Vought F-8U Crusader at the Patuxent base that got him back into flying.

"On the Verge Of Unconsciousness"

During his test-pilot assignment at Patuxent River Naval Air Station, John Glenn had to push the flying power of early models of new airplanes as hard as possible. He gives one example of this dangerous work in his book, John Glenn: A Memoir.

"I was at forty-four thousand feet over the Atlantic, getting ready to run one of the last of our high-altitude firing sequences. I flew into the test area and squeezed the trigger, and as the cannons fired, the canopy seal blew. One second I was in the pressurized equivalent of ten thousand feet of altitude, the next at an unpressurized forty-four thousand feet. At the same moment, the oxygen regulator went. I routinely switched to emergency backup.

I assumed that having weathered the near-explosive decompression, everything was under control. The first clue I had that the emergency backup had also failed was when my eyesight started deteriorating rapidly. Large patches of black started to float in my vision. I recognized the symptoms of oxygen deprivation. The oxygen regulator and its emergency function were virtually fail-safe. They never went out together. But this time they had.

I was eight miles high, with only a few seconds of vision left, and not many more of consciousness.

There was one backup left. A small bottle in my parachute pack, connected to my oxygen mask by a rubber tube, contained ten minutes of oxygen for high-altitude bailouts. I held my breath and put the plane into a steep dive as I groped for the 'little green apple.'—that green-painted, golf-ball-sized wooden ball at the end of a wire cable that would trigger this last-ditch supply. The black patches painted my vision down to nearly nothing. My lungs were bursting, and my system begged for oxygen. I was on the verge of unconsciousness when my hand closed around the wooden ball. I pulled it, exhaled in a gasp, and drew oxygen into my lungs again.

Seconds later my vision began to return and I pulled out of the dive. I took the little green apple home that night as a souvenir of survival; I still have it."

In 1956 air force planes had set a cross-country speed record of flying coast to coast in three hours and forty-five minutes. Glenn decided he could beat that record and test a new airplane as well. So, as biographer Carroll says, "He began a one-man lobbying effort to get authorization for a test flight to break the cross-country speed record set by the air force."[40]

Glenn was well prepared to request the opportunity for this transcontinental race, which he called Project Bullet. From his work with the Chance Vought plane, he knew that the Crusader could fly more than 750 miles per hour, much faster than the 586 miles per hour of a bullet. Navigating his own flight path, he plotted the procedures for refueling in the air to save time. "I sat at home and doodled out the figures and drew up some graphs and charts," Glenn told Frank Van Riper. "Then I refined my data, got some engineering figures from Chance Vought and . . . finally it looked pretty good. I went to the admiral on it and that's how the whole thing started."[41]

After four tries, Glenn's plan, Project Bullet, was approved and his flight was scheduled for July 16, 1957. As a concession to the navy's request for a backup and to satisfy the competition between the two branches of service, a tandem flight by navy lieutenant commander Charles F. Demmler was authorized.

SUPERSONIC ACHIEVEMENT

Glenn's carefully mapped route began in California at Los Alamitos Naval Air Station, located north of Long Beach, and ended at Floyd Bennett Field in Brooklyn, New York. Checkpoints every three and a half minutes would mark his progress. Airborne refueling was scheduled at Albuquerque, New Mexico; Olathe, Kansas; and Indianapolis, Indiana.

The precision flying required for refueling proved to be the crucial aspect of Glenn's success as well as the deciding factor in Demmler's failure. Unable to carry enough fuel for the three-thousand-mile flight, the plane would have to land if refueling were incomplete. Van Riper explains the process:

> The maneuver required flawless flying. For that critical procedure, Glenn reduced speed and dropped from 50,000 to 25,000 feet at the moment of rendezvous. He approached the [refueling] tanker—"an old prop plane," . . . at an exact 205 knots. The maneuver had to be accomplished gently. With a mistimed approach the drogue [anchor] trailing from the tanker might wrap itself around the [plane's] wing. A poor withdrawal could jerk the hose from the tanker and leave it stuck in the jet.[42]

Glenn's precision was clearly superior to Demmler's. He was a mere twenty seconds behind schedule at Albuquerque and on time at Olathe. Demmler failed to connect with his tanker over Albuquerque, thus dropping out of the race.

Glenn arrived at New York's Floyd Bennett Field 3 hours, 23 minutes, and 8.4 seconds after he had left California, not even the 4 hours he needed to obtain

Breaking the Sound Barrier

During the publicity tour that followed Project Bullet, Glenn explained the experience to his audiences. Part of that story is excerpted in Glenn: The Astronaut Who Would Be President, *by Frank Van Riper.*

"The course was not intentionally planned to go over New Concord. It just happened to be right on course. My mother had told some of the other people about it. They couldn't see me, of course, but they knew roughly the time I'd be coming by there.

Well, apparently, when I went supersonic, even though I was at about 40,000 feet and heading up, I was dragging enough of a shock wave cone behind me that when I went over the town there was a big double boom—whomp-whomp!! One of the old women up the street, Mrs. Gillogly, I think, called mother and said: 'Oh, Mrs. Glenn, Johnny dropped a bomb! Johnny dropped a bomb!' . . .

Flying at 1,000 miles an hour, you don't feel speed as much as you do driving 70 miles an hour down the highway. You don't have much spare time for thinking. Your speed varies 12 to 15 miles a minute. Every three-and-a-half minutes another check point comes up. By the time you check against your chart, it's time to do it all over again!

The flight was real fine. . . . No strain at all. . . . I flew coast to coast, but I didn't even make my [four hours of] flight time [needed to earn my flight pay] for the month."

John Glenn poses next to his plane following his record-breaking flight across the United States.

flight pay. The time, experts said, was even faster than a bullet's would have been and 22 minutes faster than the air force record.

Following his well-publicized landing at Floyd Bennett Field, Glenn became an instant celebrity. He took a publicity tour around the country, and Brigadier General C. A. Roberts presented him with his sixth Distinguished Flying Cross during a Labor Day celebration in New Concord, Ohio. He was the *New York Times'* "Man in the News" and appeared on the radio and on television shows in New York. The fame, however, was short lived. As Carroll writes, "Soon the cheering stopped. . . . The fastest pilot in America returned to his desk in Washington D.C."[43]

A RUSSIAN SHOCKER: *SPUTNIK,* OCTOBER 4, 1957

Not quite three months after Glenn returned to Washington, D.C., Russia succeeded in lifting a satellite, *Sputnik,* into orbit around Earth, eclipsing the achievement of Project Bullet. The rocket used to launch *Sputnik* made Americans and the U.S. government fearful of the Communists' increasing capabilities in space, and as a result, their military power. Says Van Riper, the Russians "now had the capacity to hurl their recently developed atomic bomb at the U.S. on an intercontinental ballistic missile."[44]

People all across the country began to dread an all-out nuclear war, and President

THE STRUGGLE FOR A COLLEGE DEGREE

Although John Glenn received both an undergraduate degree and an honorary doctorate from Muskingum College, in Glenn: The Astronaut Who Would Be President, *Frank Van Riper claims that Glenn's twenty-year lack of a college degree was "a sore point with him as well as with his alma mater, Muskingum College." Here, he quotes Glenn on the issue.*

"Frankly, I had more than enough credits for a college degree. In fact, I probably had enough for a masters, based on all the academic work I'd done at Patuxent, as well as college-level course work I had done right after World War II through the Armed Forces Institute. Around that time, I had also gone to the University of Maryland extension division two or three nights a week at the Pentagon.

I had transferred all this back to Muskingum, but they still wouldn't give me a degree. They held it up on a [state] residency requirement, of all things! I'd spent the first 20 years of my life there, and they still stymied it on that."

Dwight D. Eisenhower scaled up the government's space program. According to *New York Times* movie reviewer Vincent Canby, "The United States [began a] hysterical drive first to catch up with the Soviet Union's space program and then to surpass it."[45]

At first, American attempts to get into space seemed dismally inferior to the Soviet Union's. One American-made Vanguard rocket exploded on the launch pad in full view of the national television audience. Nevertheless, the U.S. satellite *Explorer I* was launched on January 31, 1958, three months after *Sputnik*.

A National Space Project

As an officer in the Bureau of Aeronautics during the administration of President Eisenhower, Glenn heard rumors about the president's move to compete with the Soviet space program. He went on to investigate and soon found out about the National Aeronautics and Space Administration (NASA), established as a civilian program on October 5, 1958, for the peaceful exploration of space.

NASA's mission, researching aerodynamics (the science of objects moving through air) and developing rockets, aircraft, and manned and unmanned satellites, greatly appealed to Glenn. He was especially interested in NASA's plans for manned spaceflights. According to Van Riper,

> He [Glenn] hungered for the assignment the moment he heard of it but . . .

The launch of a Russian satellite, Sputnik, *in October 1957, inspired the creation of a space program in the United States.*

he anxiously wondered whether he could meet the program's criteria. There were four obstacles to surmount, any one of which could have disqualified him. One, in fact, almost did.

By the standards NASA set, Glenn was considerably overweight at 208 pounds, as his round face and thick thighs gave evidence. He was also 37 years old, a mere two years under the cutoff age of 39, but still considerably older than most of the candidates likely to apply. He also lacked a college degree. The criteria were clear on this point. And lastly, he was too tall. A 5'11" cutoff had been set in order to ensure sufficient legroom in a cramped space capsule.[46]

COMPETING FOR A NASA ASSIGNMENT

Glenn immediately set out to meet NASA's requirements. The height restriction was reportedly the most difficult obstacle for the six-foot Glenn. His friend Tom Miller told Van Riper, "In order to meet the requirements for the astronaut program, Glenn literally tried to shrink himself down to size. . . . Every evening for at least two hours . . . John would sit and walk around the house with about twelve inches of books strapped to his head, trying to get himself smaller."[47] (Actually, Glenn says, he was five foot eleven to start with, and his friend was only joking.)

Glenn addressed the other requirements, too. He undertook a fitness routine to get himself into shape. Working out by

Here, John Glenn is pictured (third from the right) with the other six chosen astronauts.

jumping on a trampoline, swimming, lifting barbells, and running, he got down to 167 pounds. To satisfy the education requirements, he corresponded with Muskingum College and the University of Maryland, certain that the courses he had taken over the years would fulfill the degree requirement without his having to spend four years on campus. And in addition to all of the courses that he had taken in the service, he held that his age and experience were assets.

Glenn also got a break when NASA officials realized that their candidate pool was not wholly representative of the U.S. military. As Robert B. Voas, the psychologist on the selection committee, relates, "It wasn't until we had selected almost all the 110 candidates that it was called to my attention that we didn't have any Marines. . . . So we had to make a quick contact with the Marine Corps and they found two pilots who fit the requirements. One was John Glenn."[48]

After a severe screening and testing regimen, NASA chose an astronaut team that included several branches of the U.S. military. The seven members were Colonel John Glenn of the marines; Lieutenant Commanders Alan B. Shepard Jr. and Walter M. "Wally" Schirra of the navy; and Captains Virgil A. "Gus" Grissom, Malcolm Scott Carpenter, Leroy Gordon Cooper Jr., and Donald K. "Deke" Slayton of the air force. Over the next three years these men symbolized the American space program. They traveled thousands of miles to learn about and supervise the production of the various systems of Project Mercury, the first American manned spaceflight.

Chapter
4 The First American Astronaut to Orbit Earth

When the seven Project Mercury astronauts arrived at Langley Air Force Base on April 8, 1959, they met first with Dr. Robert R. Gilruth, the director of NASA's Space Task Group. Gilruth hardly needed to emphasize the danger of space travel, for a Vanguard satellite launch explosion had recently shown how much the scientists had to learn about rockets and rocket fuel. Glenn quotes Gilruth in his memoir: "Project Mercury isn't a continuation of anything. Nobody's ever gone into space before. It's completely new, it's untried, there are many uncertainties ahead. If for any reason whatsoever you decide it's not for you, you can go back to your respective services with no questions asked."[49] No one left. Gilruth went on to emphasize that NASA was sincere in asking for the astronauts' input on any problems they saw with their instruments. Everything had to work perfectly.

Participation in Project Mercury required that Glenn and the other astronauts commit themselves to a tough training program designed by navy psychologist Lieutenant Robert B. Voas. This program demanded that the astronauts test their minds and bodies, as well as their experimental spacecraft, to see how far they could stretch themselves and their equipment under three stresses: liftoff, weightlessness in orbit, and landing.

THE TRAINING MACHINES

To train for liftoff, the astronauts rode machines in which they were shaken, buffeted, and subjected to unbelievable pressure, noise, and heat, such as might be experienced when the Atlas or Redstone rocket boosters exploded beneath them. One training machine, the Wheel, or centrifuge, was, according to Glenn, a lot like a gondola at the end of a fifty-foot arm circling around rapidly, then slowing so rapidly that the pressure forced the rider's eyeballs in and out of his eye sockets. The Wheel simulated gravity up to sixteen times its natural pull, such as would result from the launch's sudden acceleration. At seven miles per second the astronauts would travel a little more than 113 miles above the surface of Earth.

The training equipment showed the men that liftoff could cause unconsciousness. They learned that they needed to be on their backs, exerting muscle pressure on their abdomens to keep from blacking out. Glenn, who was in charge of cockpit design, had to help plan the seats (which are more like beds) in which the astronauts would sit during liftoff and would spend their time during orbit. It was his responsibility to plan every aspect of the tiny room, which barely held the astronaut and his instrument panel.

Weightlessness in flight, the second unknown, was the focus of other training. In one machine the men experienced something like the suspension that happens when a body is beyond the pull of gravity. Although the machine could simulate weightlessness for only a few seconds, the men could be tested to see if their bodily functions were impaired.

The inside of the space capsule was an artificial environment that had to support them outside the atmosphere. To test the environmental control systems that would sustain them during orbit, Wally Schirra supervised the training. The astronauts spent hours lying down while technicians checked and rechecked the tubes,

The Vanguard satellite launch explosion proved that the United States had much to learn about rockets and the dangers of space exploration.

The training device pictured here called the centrifuge simulated gravity up to sixteen times its natural pull and prepared the Project Mercury astronauts for the feeling of launching into space.

wiring, connections, and instruments of their pressure suits. They had to study their reactions to oxygen deprivation, heat, cold, isolation, and silence. When minutes of testing turned into hours, as Glenn recalls, the astronauts discovered one unforeseen difficulty:

> No urine collection device had been designed for use inside the space suit. The early missions were going to be only fifteen minutes long, and nobody had thought that the testing and other delays might stretch on as long as they did. To break for a pit stop was often impossible in the middle of a test. It meant getting out of the pressure suit, which was no quick and easy task, and then putting it on all over again. I forgot who was the first to do it, but once we realized how much time and trouble was involved, we just shrugged and let it go. You got used to it after a while, lying on your back while your thick suit underwear with its air tubes sopped up the urine as it worked its way up your back. It was preferable to bringing the whole operation to a halt.[50]

SURVIVAL PROCEDURES: A PART OF PREFLIGHT TRAINING

The Project Mercury training program tried to prepare the astronauts for the various situations they might encounter during and after their spaceflight. In John Glenn: A Memoir, *Glenn recalls his training for the possibility of the capsule landing in the desert.*

"After our classroom work, Air Force helicopters flew us sixty miles east to a remote desert of hot sand, cactus, and sagebrush, and left us. We scattered to individual sites, where we were to survive for three days. We had the parachutes and shrouds and the survival kits. The first thing you did was take a knife and cut a section of parachute, make a hole to stick your head through, and drape it over you for sun protection. Repeated several times, you had a version of the layered, loose-fitting costumes worn in North Africa and the Middle East. Some more of the parachute fabric went into making a cover for your head. Still more of it became your shoes, sections that were rolled up and bound to your feet with the parachute shrouds. It was an ingenious system.

Bill Douglas oversaw the desert training. We were all on our own in the desert, but Bill knew where we were and checked on each of us regularly to see if we were okay.

The instructors had told us before we went out about the debilitating effects of dehydration. I was curious about what it was like, and told Bill I wanted to try it.

He told me he'd keep an eye on me, so for the first twenty-four hours I didn't drink any water.

By then I was getting pretty low. I had dug out a little area under some sagebrush, as we had been taught to do—the subsurface temperature was a little lower, and the sagebrush with parachute fabric over it provided shade—and I was lying there as debilitated as I have ever been. When Bill showed up again, I didn't even want to raise my hand and shade my eyes to look at him as he came walking up.

Bill had brought plenty of water, and told me to drink as much as I wanted. I drank fifteen pints over the next nine hours without passing a drop. I could not believe how quickly my body had dried out, and to this day I still carry extra water if I have to drive across the desert."

A final training routine prepared the men for the return to the force of gravity during the recovery of the space vehicle. The routine simulated the twisting and turning the engineers thought might happen while slowing down from the orbiting speed of 17,500 miles per hour to the 250 miles per hour needed for splashdown. A machine, the Multiple Axis Space Test Inertia Facility (MASTIF) gave them a three-way spin. Gus Grissom describes the machine's action: "The purpose of MASTIF was to get us revolving and tumbling and spinning on a dizzy ride in all three directions at once in order to see how well we could manipulate the three-axis controls to connect the fantastic combination of yawing, pitching and rolling which the machine could throw at us."[51]

Despite the rigorous training methods and state-of-the-art tracking equipment, it was still possible for the space capsule not to land where the scientists expected it to. The astronauts had to be prepared for that as well. In case the capsule should go off course and come down in uncharted territory—the ocean, jungle, or desert—the men had to learn and practice survival skills at the Chesapeake Bay, the Gulf of Mexico, and the desert near Stead Air Force Base in Nevada. Underwater exercises to check recovery procedures and desert survival training were just two of the activities in which the men participated.

For Glenn, there was an added training regime. Since he tended to gain weight, the program had too much sitting and inactivity for him. Therefore, in addition to the astronaut training, he mapped out a two-mile run to keep the pounds off. He also worked out by waterskiing with the other astronauts. Mindful of the need for top physical condition, he even quit smoking his occasional pipeful of tobacco.

A PUBLIC JOB

As the 1950s came to a close, the race to put a man in space became very competitive, with the Soviet Union and the United States battling for the first liftoff of a manned vehicle. Following *Sputnik*, the Soviets launched several other satellites into space while the United States struggled to catch up. Then Project Mercury got a boost, when John F. Kennedy's 1960 presidential campaign included his promise to put a man on the moon by the end of the decade if he were elected.

As a result of the fast-paced and competitive race, massive media attention thrust the astronauts and the jobs they were performing into the public eye. Everything involved with Project Mercury, successful or not, was reported, and NASA's public image went from good to bad according to the story of the day.

With public favor going up and down, Congress was reluctant to authorize the nearly $400 million budget needed to pay for the astronauts' preparation and space equipment. In response to the fickle public support and Congress's indecision, NASA orchestrated a publicity campaign to improve its image. NASA officials signed an exclusive contract with *Life* magazine for the astronauts' stories. This contract gave NASA a good deal of control over Project Mercury news. Outside of routine press conferences, only *Life* reporters could interview the astronauts and their families. This arrangement offered the American public a one-sided version of the Project Mercury story and made heroes of the astronauts involved in it.

THE BATTLE FOR PRIVACY

For Glenn, the *Life* contract was a gift. On weekends when he was at Langley Air Force Base in Virginia, he could drive to the Virginia home he and Annie had established after his return from Korea. His son Dave, at thirteen, and daughter Lyn, at twelve, were involved in school, and Annie

President John F. Kennedy was a major supporter of the U.S. space program.

had friends nearby to turn to if she needed help with anything. Thanks to the *Life* contract, Glenn could catch up on their activities without intrusion from other reporters.

These weekend visits also provided time for Glenn to discuss with his wife and children his training and everything else that he was doing in Project Mercury. It was important to him that Annie understand the time he had to spend at work. He could also give his own answers to the family's questions about the inevitable risks he was taking.

Weekends at Arlington were not always possible, however. In addition to their work at Langley Air Force Base, Glenn and the other astronauts had onsite jobs far away at Cape Canaveral, east of Orlando, Florida, where their manned flights would originate. In Florida the only leisure accommodations within miles were at the Starlite Motel in Cocoa Beach. The motel's manager, Henri Landwirth, liked to visit with the astronauts and encouraged them to come there to get away from the stress of the base. Later, when Landwirth accepted a job at the Cocoa Beach Holiday Inn he invited the astronauts and their families as well. Glenn brought Annie, Lyn, and Dave down to Florida on weekends, where they could relax together, go on fishing or sailboat excursions, walks along the beach, and swims in the hotel pool. Some of the other astronauts, however, did not use that time to spend time with their wives and families. Instead, some became involved in extramarital affairs, relationships that Glenn considered inappropriate.

A Question of Public or Private

During team meetings at Langley Air Force Base, the astronauts discussed their feelings and attitudes about anything that affected their work on Project Mercury. At these meetings, Glenn occasionally brought up his views on drinking and casual sex. To his peers, Glenn seemed overly eager to promote his family and religious values. To Glenn, his intentions were simply meant to avert bad press. As he writes, "Of course, what each person did in his private time was his business. But *Life* magazine was painting us all in glowing terms, and I thought that one story tarnishing that image was all it would take to put the whole program in jeopardy."[52]

The media, as Glenn suspected, was more than happy to bring up possible problems associated with Project Mercury. Some reporters suggested that perhaps pilots were unnecessary; primates and automatic instruments would be better and cheaper. Others went so far as to seek out astronauts in compromising situations.

One such situation arose early in the morning while the team was in San Diego for a meeting with rocket engineers. Glenn's friend and official NASA spokesman Colonel John Powers called Glenn at two in the morning to report that the editor of a West Coast paper had accepted photographs and an exposé on one of the team members. The photographer had followed the astronaut and a woman from San Diego to Tijuana,

Mexico, taking pictures that could prove to be damaging to the astronauts' and NASA's reputation. Powers felt sure the story had high potential to spoil the idealistic image Glenn valued so highly.

Despite Powers's doubts to the contrary, Glenn thought something could be done to stop the story. Glenn recalls,

> I called the reporter and photographer. I called the editor and got him out of bed. I talked about why it was important to the country and the program that the story not run. I talked about the godless Communists and how they were ahead of us, and how the press had to let us get back in the space race. I pulled out all the stops.
>
> When my alarm rang in the morning, I got up and went straight to the hotel newsstand. The story wasn't in the paper. To this day, and knowing the press much better now, I'm still amazed that it didn't run.[53]

Scott Carpenter, one of the seven members of the Mercury team, trains at Langley Air Force Base in Virginia.

Major Gagarin's Conversation with Chairman Khrushchev

Chairman Nikita Khrushchev of the Soviet Union received Major Yuri Gagarin's report of his successful orbit at 1:00 P.M. Moscow time, April 12, 1961. Here is part of their conversation, which appeared in the April 13 issue of the Moscow newspaper, Pravda, *and is reprinted in* The First Man in Space: The Record of Yuri Gagarin's First Venture into Cosmic Space, a Collection of Translations from Soviet Press Reports.

"Khrushchev: I warmly greet and congratulate you, dear Yuri Alexeyevich! You are the first man in the world to have traveled in space. With your exploit you have glorified our country, and shown courage and heroism in carrying out such an important task. With your exploit you have immortalized yourself as the first person to penetrate into space.

Tell me, Yuri Alexeyevich, how did you feel in flight? How did this first space flight proceed?

Gagarin: I felt well. The flight was most successful. All the instruments of the spaceship worked faultlessly. During the flight I could see the earth from that great height. I could see the seas, mountains, big cities, rivers and forests.

Khrushchev: Then you felt well?

Gagarin: That's right, Nikita Sergeyevich. I felt fine in the spaceship, quite at home. Thank you once again for your kind message of congratulations and for your good wishes on the successful flight.

Krushchev: I am glad to hear your voice and to greet you. I shall be happy to meet you in Moscow. You and I, together with our whole people, shall celebrate this great exploit in the conquest of space. Let the whole world see what our country is capable of, what our great people and our Soviet science can do.

Gagarin: Let all countries catch up with us now!

Khrushchev: Quite right! I am glad to hear your voice sound so cheerful and confident, and to know that you are in such high spirits! You are quite right: Let the capitalist countries catch up with our country, which has blazed the trail into outer space and sent up the world's first astronaut. We are all proud of this great victory."

Nor did Glenn leave it at that. The next day he angrily confronted the astronauts. Only Scott Carpenter backed Glenn, agreeing that the astronauts were role models and, as such, had certain responsibilities. The others would only begrudgingly admit that they were going to make aviation history and that their private lives would be part of the record.

The incident left a lasting impression. Although some of the astronauts changed their behavior, the relationships among the seven of them were strained. Regardless, Glenn felt they had neither the time nor the energy for bickering. For Project Mercury to be a success, everyone would have to work together. He said it was "a vast collaborative enterprise, its lofty goals bringing out the best in everybody from the assembly line up. We astronauts may have had our differences, but they didn't affect the teamwork that was required."[54]

WHO WOULD BE FIRST?

As the actual flight deadlines neared and the astronauts began to wonder who would be chosen to man the first space capsule, some of the team members did let those differences fuel some competition. Glenn, like the others, wanted to be first. The issue was ultimately decided by a peer vote, and Glenn's actions regarding the private lives of the astronauts proved to be a key factor in the result. Alan Shepard was voted to take the first preorbital flight, Gus Grissom the second; John Glenn was third.

As it turned out, however, none of the American astronauts was first. The Soviets won that race. On April 13, 1961, Major Yuri A. Gagarin of the Soviet Union orbited Earth before any of NASA's manned vehicles left the ground. Gagarin's 108-minute orbit galvanized the Project Mercury team, and NASA, in the interest of time, actually eliminated some of the tests that had been planned.

Less than one month later, on May 5, 1961, Shepard became the first American to go above the atmosphere. His launch was covered by world television, and his suborbital flight showed that the launch rocket had enough power to carry the capsule into orbit. Shepard's experience also showed that the space capsule needed a window.

When Grissom made the second suborbital flight on July 19, 1961, not only was a window added, but Grissom also had a urine collection device. Grissom's capsule splashed down on target, but his flight also turned up other flaws in the equipment. While he waited for the recovery crew, the automatic release on the hatch blew, and water entered the capsule. Grissom escaped through the open hatch, but his suit filled with water and he almost drowned. The vehicle was lost.

GLENN'S TURN

Glenn was next in line. Eleven dates were set before the actual liftoff took place. Weather or the failure of some small piece of hardware always interfered. "It would be announced," says Glenn, "that Glenn is going on such and such date, and then no,

John Glenn, pictured (left) in his flight suit, won fame for his orbital flight in an Atlas rocket like the one pictured on the right.

it's been canceled because of something or other. Once I was on my way to the pad in the van when the flight was canceled. . . . We couldn't get this thing [the flight] off. It was almost like it was designed for suspense by Hollywood."[55]

The suspense affected everyone around the base. For example, Leo DeOrsey, Glenn's business adviser, thought the risks necessitated life insurance for Glenn. Not finding a company he could afford, DeOrsey finally wrote out a one-hundred-thousand-dollar personal check to Annie

and gave it to a friend who agreed to deliver it if Glenn died or to return it to DeOrsey if Glenn returned safely.

Media coverage and celebrations were also put on hold eleven times. Reporters swarmed around Cape Canaveral for every scheduled liftoff. Henri Landwirth had the bakers at the Holiday Inn in Cocoa Beach make a nine-hundred-pound celebration cake shaped like the space capsule. As the delays continued, Landwirth kept the huge cake cool with a battery of fans. Finally, on February 20, 1962,

John Glenn donned his space suit for the three-orbit flight that made U.S. history.

A HISTORIC LIFTOFF

For Glenn, the day began at 1:30 A.M. with a weather report and a medical exam. As he put on his space suit, he made jokes and seemed completely at ease with the idea of traveling into space.

At 6:00 A.M. searchlights lit the top of the Atlas rocket, and reporters and spectators lined every available observation point on Cape Canaveral as Glenn boarded his space capsule, called *Friendship 7*. Nearly four hours later, at 9:47 A.M. countdown reached zero and the rocket exploded. Glenn describes the sensation as "a solid and exhilarating surge of up and away."[56] The shaking, spinning, yawing, pitching, and rolling for which training had prepared him were minimal and lasted less than a minute. As the capsule entered its orbit, Glenn writes, "there was no sensation of speed" and "only a slight bump" as the booster tower separated. Glenn reached orbit 5 minutes and 1.4 seconds after liftoff, with "a barely noticeable sensation of tumbling forward when the capsule separated."[57]

HARROWING MEDIA COVERAGE

The liftoff and orbit of *Friendship 7* on February 20, 1962, was a worldwide media event. The minute-by-minute television coverage, seen by virtually every American, was as historic as the orbit itself. The flight, however, was not problem-free. As Glenn flew through space, a warning light at mission control indicated that his capsule might have a loose heat shield. Such a malfunction could cause Glenn's capsule to burn upon reentering the atmosphere. NASA officials chose not to tell Glenn, fearing the knowledge might compromise his mission.

Newscasters, however, told the listening audience of the possible problem. But Glenn's reassuring voice, recorded in space headquarters minute by minute, alleviated some of the concern. He felt fine. He saw the curve of Earth, a beautiful sight, and operated controls manually to make up for a malfunction in the automatic steering. One by one, Glenn noted the places he passed, checking in with his colleagues around the world in Nigeria, Zanzibar, the Indian Ocean, Australia, California, and Texas.

NASA officials, however, were still concerned about the troublesome light. Moments before Glenn was scheduled to begin the reentry process and lose communications contact, he was asked to turn the warning light on and off manually. Nothing happened. At approximately 12:39 P.M. (Eastern Time) the expected communications cutoff began, and *Friendship 7* reentered the atmosphere.

For the television audience the glowing capsule and the blackout of communications were fearsome. As for Glenn, he could only do his job and wait to see what would happen. In an article published in *National Geographic* magazine, Robert B. Voas narrates those moments:

Is the Heat Shield Loose?

During Glenn's first orbit, signals at NASA control seemed to indicate that his heat shield had come loose. The minutes before he returned to Earth were tense for everyone involved. In a Life *magazine article entitled, "If You're Shook Up You Shouldn't Be There," Glenn recalled the moments before landing.*

"[Fellow astronaut] Al Shepard came on [the radio] to explain that Mercury Control had had an indication by telemetry earlier in the flight that my heat shield might have come loose. If this were true, I could be in for some difficulty. The heat shield . . . was the only thing that stood between me and disaster as we came through the atmosphere. . . .

As we started to heat up on re-entry, I could feel something let go on the blunt end of the capsule behind me. . . . Then I began to see a bright orange glow building up around the capsule. . . . Right away I could see flaming chunks go flying by the window. Some of them were as big as six to eight inches across. I could hear them bump against the capsule behind me before they took off, and I thought that the heat shield might be tearing apart. This was a bad moment. But I knew that if that was what was really happening it would all be over shortly and there was nothing I could do about it. So I kept on with what I'd been doing—trying to keep the capsule under control—and sweated it out."

Outside the window [Glenn] sees an orange glow. Its brilliance grows.

Now the orange color intensifies. Suddenly large flaming pieces of metal come rushing back past the window. What can they be? He thought the retropack was gone. For a moment he feels that the capsule itself must be burning and breaking up. Deceleration holds him, pressing him back into the seat, or he would involuntarily rise up, expecting at any moment to feel the first warmth as the heat burns through the capsule to his back. But it doesn't come.[58]

"Just a Normal Day in Space"

Splashdown and recovery of *Friendship 7* proceeded pretty much as scheduled. Glenn, as reported by *Life* magazine, "felt a moment of 'cautious apprehension' when he thought his heat shield was gone,"[59] but he kept his cool, checking his responses, practicing his typical self-control, watching the capsule's parachute unfold behind him, hitting the water, and waiting in the hot capsule.

The recovery ship arrived within minutes, and a helicopter retrieved the capsule and set it on deck. Glenn opened the hatch, stepped out, and was handed a glass of iced tea. He looked at his space capsule proudly. It had come through the fire. After changing clothes, he spoke with President Kennedy by phone. By

---

WHY GLENN DID NOT GO TO THE MOON

On February 25, 1962, James Reston titled his regular New York Times *column, "Is the Moon Really Worth John Glenn?" Through his tongue-in-cheek request that Glenn be transferred to Washington, D.C., he reveals a sincere admiration for Glenn's character.*

"What we constantly observe, we tend to copy. What we admire and reward, we perpetuate. This is why John Glenn himself is almost as important as his flight into outer space, for he dramatized before the eyes of the whole nation the noblest qualities of the human spirit.

Outside of the . . . cowboy movies . . . courage, modesty, quiet patriotism, love of family and religious faith are not exactly the predominant themes . . . these days. Yet Glenn dramatized them all coast to coast and around the world.

This was no insensitive robot who landed here from the heavens yesterday morning, but a warm and thoughtful human being: natural, orderly, considerate and, at times, quietly amusing and even eloquent.

His departure from Cape Canaveral in a blaze of orange fire was a technical triumph, but his return was a human triumph. When he came back and saw his lovely wife, Annie, he put his head on her shoulder and cried. Thereafter nothing ruffled him, not the President, or the clamorous press, or the whirring cameras, or the eager shouting crowds. . . .

Outer space is a long way to go to discover a new generation of leaders of men, but if we have to recruit them there, why not? Human weightlessness is almost our major problem in Washington and, since these astronauts know more about it than anybody else, maybe a couple of them should be transferred to the thin hot air of the capital."

sunset he was shuttled to an aircraft carrier and was given a medical exam and a steak dinner.

A detailed medical examination and a two-day debriefing followed at the medical center on Grand Turk Island. As time passed, Glenn's response to questions about his flight became more and more relaxed. When finally asked about any unusual activity, Glenn's response was simple: "Just a normal day in space."[60]

THE NATION HONORS HIM

By the time Glenn left the debriefing center, accompanied by Vice President Lyndon B. Johnson, he began to realize that he had become an instant national hero. Annie and the family were at Cape Canaveral to join him in a parade. President Kennedy arrived and presented Glenn with NASA's Distinguished Service Medal. Landwirth served his month-old cake at a huge reception, and

After Glenn's successful space flight, he became a national hero and received many honors, including a parade in New York City.

Glenn finally got away for the weekend with his family.

After the weekend, President Kennedy returned to Cape Canaveral on Monday, February 24, to escort Glenn to Washington, D.C. As he visited with the president, Glenn was impressed by Kennedy's personality. He wrote later, "I saw that the Kennedy charisma could move millions to contribute to something I thought was vital—a democracy of energized participation in which people shared their talents with the nation."[61]

In an unprecedented show of support for the astronauts and NASA, Congress called a joint session. Ambassadors, foreign officials, even the Supreme Court justices gathered at the Capitol in an event usually reserved for heads of state. Glenn introduced his teammates and his family, and the House and the Senate gave him a standing ovation for his seventeen-minute speech, which basically asked Congress to continue supporting NASA's program.

Another week of celebrations followed, climaxing on Sunday, March 1, 1962, when New York gave all of the astronauts a huge ticker-tape parade down Broadway. Finally, on Tuesday, March 3, Glenn returned to New Concord, Ohio, where fifty thousand people (thirty times the town's normal population) followed his motorcade down Main Street. Sixteen hundred people crowded into the Muskingum College gym as Mayor James Taylor announced that the gym had been renamed for Glenn, along with a section of highway and a new high school.

Awards kept rolling in during the next weeks. Vice President Johnson pre-

sented Glenn with the Goddard Award, and the National Geographic Society awarded him the Hubbard Medal "for extraordinary contributions to scientific knowledge of the world and beyond as a pioneer in exploring the ocean of space."[62] He was also named "Father of the Year" and, along with his fellow astronauts, received the Catholic War Veterans' Celtic Cross. The U.S. Marine Corps named Glenn "Best Aviator of the Year" with the Cunningham Award, and the Pentagon awarded him astronaut wings. Furthermore, NASA officially acknowledged that the mission could not have been completed without Glenn's piloting.

A Protégé of President Kennedy

Soon after his return from space, Glenn started hoping for his next assignment. NASA was focusing attention on Project Apollo, the trip to the Moon, and Glenn wanted to be involved in the mission. However, his hopes diminished as one after another of the Apollo astronauts were announced, and he was not included. Instead, there were invitations to visit the Kennedys.

The situation was confusing and difficult for Glenn to understand. As biographer Peter N. Carroll writes, the president had become very fond of John Glenn and also saw the influence the astronaut had over the American people. Kennedy worried that if something happened to Glenn on a future spaceflight, support for the space program might disappear. Carroll explains,

> Glenn . . . became a friend of the Kennedy's, attending the famous pool parties at Robert and Ethel Kennedy's Hickory Hill [home] and sailing aboard the president's yacht. . . . In January 1963 NASA assigned Glenn to Project Apollo, the effort to place a man on the moon. At age forty-one he still dreamed of another mission into space. He did not know that President Kennedy, fearing the effects on public morale of a tragic accident, had ordered NASA to keep him on the ground.[63]

The intense training and dedication of Glenn and the other astronauts had carried not only the United States but also the entire world into a new era. It was not mere heroics that had made John Glenn a household name. It was the promise his accomplishment offered. He had proved that an ordinary fellow from Ohio could explore outer space; the age of space travel had begun.

5 A Hero with Other Work to Do

Throughout his life John Glenn had engineered much of his own success. From getting his parents' permission to fly to placing himself in line for one of the seven positions in Project Mercury, Glenn was the major mover in his career. But during the spring and summer following his orbital flight, that career seemed at a standstill.

Part of the time Glenn was involved in moving his family from Arlington to Houston, Texas, where the Manned Space Center was transferring its Langley Air Force Base operations. Another large part of his time was taken up by public relations activities for NASA. In fact, publicity and nationwide travel claimed so much of his attention that he could not do the research, testing, or even flying necessary to be eligible for military promotion.

Furthermore, Glenn's personal life was affected by the usual trappings of celebrity. Routine shopping trips were time-consuming for him and any family member who happened to be along, as he was a sucker for anyone who asked for his autograph. The job of answering his mail grew exponentially as schoolchildren around the country and ordinary people around the world expressed their awe at his accomplishments.

THE KENNEDY INFLUENCE

Realizing he would not be a part of NASA's lunar program, Glenn began to listen to another call—the call to elected public service. He could trace his interest in public office to his high-school student council days and more recently to his contact with President Kennedy. In fact, some observers, such as biographer Frank Van Riper, believed that the president was actually priming Glenn for the seat of Stephen Young, the incumbent Democratic senator from Ohio. Glenn's popularity, it seemed, might help Kennedy's cause in the strongly Republican state. Already, says Van Riper, Wayne B. Hays, an Ohio congressman friendly to Kennedy, "had let it be known that he had been 'authorized' to discuss an 'ambassadorship' for Young if he would step aside."[64]

It was not meant to be, however, and events took a violent turn when President Kennedy was shot in Dallas on November 22, 1963. The assassination, Van Riper says, "removed the only person with the

John Glenn and President John F. Kennedy stand beside the space capsule in which Glenn orbited the earth.

power to make the 1964 election risk-free by persuading Young to step aside. In pragmatic political terms, Kennedy's death meant the deal was off."[65]

Glenn was shaken by Kennedy's death. He had lost a good friend and political ally and was suddenly forced to reevaluate his own political future. "In the death of the president," writes Peter N. Carroll, "Glenn saw reminders of his own survivals—in World War II, in Korea, the red smoke above the Atlantic—and he felt an obligation to justify the sacrifices of those less lucky than himself."[66]

Glenn spent the year following Kennedy's death contemplating his possibilities in the field of public service. Despite his desire to hold office, Glenn saw many obstacles to a successful career in politics. For one thing, both Robert F. Kennedy, the late president's brother, and President Lyndon B. Johnson told Glenn

that there was not enough time to build a campaign. More importantly, his career as a military man, respectful of the military law that prohibited uniformed servicemen from expressing political preferences, prolonged his delays; he could not freely campaign unless he resigned from the marines and his assignment to NASA. Above all, he was inexperienced and a political unknown. He had never made known any party leanings and had to admit that he usually split his votes between Republicans and Democrats.

GLENN'S NEW MISSION

By the end of 1963, it nevertheless became clear to Glenn that he could not give up on a political career without trying. On January 15, 1964, Robert R. Gilruth, director of the Manned Space Center in Houston, announced that Colonel Glenn had been relieved of his assignment at NASA. Two days later, having also firmed up his intentions to resign from the marines and in spite of Kennedy's and Johnson's advice, Glenn announced that he was a Democratic candidate for the U.S. Senate, vying for the seat of Stephen Young. Political experience would come, he contended, and he hoped to advance the Democratic platform as articulated by President Johnson.

Glenn began his political race with neither a plan of action nor a well-formed philosophy. In his early press conferences, he refused to make clear statements about political beliefs, at least in part because his resignation from the marines would not be effective until March. Nor did he speak

John Glenn, pictured in a NASA uniform, left NASA in 1964 and began to think seriously about running for the United States Senate.

of Project Mercury: He did not want to ride to the Senate on the roller coaster of his national fame as an astronaut. Says Carroll,

> [Glenn] believed that personal qualities, patriotism, and virtue constitute sufficient criteria for leadership and that he could learn about politics from books. In his ranch-style house in one of the newly built suburbs of Houston, near the NASA space center, he sat in his den surrounded by trophies and put himself through a crash course in political theory. He read John Kennedy's *Profiles in Courage* and Theodore White's *The Making of the President, 1960*, John Kenneth Galbraith's *The Affluent Society* and Barry Goldwater's *The Conscience of a Conservative*.[67]

All of these influences did indeed handicap Glenn's bid for office. Trying to be both conservative and liberal, he synthesized a non-ideological approach to politics based on the idea that no single group had all of the answers to the nation's problems. That seemingly indecisive stand, coupled with his unwillingness to capitalize on his hero status doomed Glenn's initial Senate race from the start.

A Freak Accident

A freak accident ended his chances completely. On February 26, 1964, barely a month after his announcement, Glenn took a campaign trip to Columbus, Ohio. While there, he noticed that a sliding mirror on the medicine cabinet in his hotel room was off its track. As he tried to reset the mirror, he shifted his weight, and the small rug on the floor slipped under his feet. He fell against the metal edge of the bathtub. He later explained,

> Suddenly I realized I was slipping, but I tried to hold on to the mirror and keep it from breaking, rather than let go and use one of my hands to break the fall. I began to spin as I fell. . . . The mirror flew from my grip and crashed to the floor. Flying pieces of glass cut my hands and face. . . . It was the toughest wallop I've ever taken. . . .
>
> I didn't pass out, but I was in a state of shock. . . . When I moved my head the least bit, it was as if the whole world were spinning upside down.[68]

Rushed to the hospital, he was diagnosed with a mild concussion. Bleeding in his inner ear caused damage to his vestibular (balance) system. The resulting dizziness and nausea were so severe that he quickly requested convalescent leave instead of retirement from the marines.

A Debtor Becomes a Millionaire

Glenn's hospitalization lasted for more than a month, but he did not formally remove his name from the Ohio Senate race. This oversight turned out to be a huge financial mistake. Glenn allowed his friends

SOME LETTERS TO JOHN GLENN

While he recovered from a bad fall in a Columbus, Ohio, hotel room, John Glenn enjoyed reading the thousands of letters he had received after orbiting Earth. Three of them are excerpted here from the book P. S. I Listened to Your Heart Beat: Letters to John Glenn.

"A high-school sophomore in Whiting, Iowa:

I am a fifteen-year old boy and a sophomore in high school. I need your advice. Ever since the launch of Sputnik I, I have read everything available on Space. I take four space magazines. I know that I want to be an astronaut. Should I join some branch of the service after graduation, like the U.S. Air Force Academy, or should I go to college and get hitched up with N.A.S.A?

From a woman who gave no address:

I want to tell you that your decision to enter the political field is one that will, I am sure, meet with the whole hearted approval of many people.

What matters is that you believe in your country and its future. . . .

I feel you have the necessary spiritual and moral courage to do this—just as you had the physical courage required for your launch into space.

I believe we need men such as you in the government—men who are dedicated to their country's greatness—men of courage and wisdom and vision.

From the Soviet ambassador to the U.S., Anatoly F. Dobrynin:

The Embassy was requested by Soviet citizen Mr. Podyrzev (Voronesh, USSR) to obtain some stamps issued in the United States in honor of you and other American astronauts with your personal autograph. The stamps will be showed at a children's exhibition.

I would appreciate very much if you could sign the envelopes enclosed herewith.

In accordance with the request of Mr. Podyrzev I am sending you herewith the stamps issued in the Soviet Union in honor of the Soviet cosmonauts which Mr. Podyrzev's son would be glad to present to you."

to continue campaigning for him in the primary election. When he finally withdrew on May 30, 1964, he owed nearly $10,000 for pamphlets and other materials, an amount almost equal to the year's convalescent leave salary. This and the fact that military pay had never been more than $17,500 a year, left him with severe financial difficulties. Surgery for Annie to relieve her endometriosis (malformation of the uterus) and Dave's enrollment at Harvard only placed additional stress on the Glenn budget.

With no definite prospect of a full recovery, Glenn began searching for employment opportunities. While he was looking, he also started reading the immense amount of mail he had received after orbiting Earth. Slowly an idea began to form: He could compile samples of the letters into a publishable book and make a little money in the process. That summer he categorized and sorted them. The book of collected letters, *P.S. I Listened to Your Heart Beat: Letters to John Glenn*, was published by World Book Encyclopedia before the end of the year.

By the time the book was completed, Glenn felt he was on his way to recovery, and he started looking for work. He still intended to end his career in the marines and began to consider other job offers. He wanted something that would permit him to travel overseas, keep up his interest in space and religious activities, and continue his volunteer work with the Boy Scouts.

In October 1964, Glenn accepted a part-time position as vice president for corporate development at the Royal Crown Cola Company. He was responsible for developing and expanding the company's international operations. Since the directors agreed not to have him sell anything (as a marine, he could not endorse products), he could use the salary of fifty-thousand dollars toward paying his campaign debts.

The job was perfectly suited for Glenn in many ways. He could combine it with consulting and making goodwill tours for NASA. He visited Germany, Holland, Italy, Spain, and Portugal, inspecting rockets. He also had plenty of time for himself, attending industrial fairs and meeting Pope Paul VI. He resumed jogging, driving, and waterskiing. He also took a jet refresher course.

Finally, on January 4, 1965, after passing a thorough physical examination, he retired honorably and without disability from twenty-three years in the U.S. Marine Corps. Royal Crown Cola, pleased that Glenn's contacts and fame had proved valuable, created a subsidiary, Royal Crown Cola International Limited, for him to head up. As its president, he and his family enjoyed an affluence far above what his military salary had afforded. The position even included the perk of a luxury apartment in New York City. Ultimately, Glenn traveled to twenty countries to establish Royal Crown franchises.

In the late 1960s Glenn accepted an additional money-making offer from his old friend Henri Landwirth. The Florida hotel manager invited Glenn to join him in a business deal building Holiday Inns. The Disney Company had just opened a new entertainment complex, called Disney

World, in Orlando. When Glenn heard the plan, to build a hotel on each of the four sides of the new park, as Landwirth later told interviewer Howard Kohn, Glenn "was eager to get involved" and "wanted very much to have greater financial security."[69] According to the deal, Landwirth and Glenn each owned 25 percent shares, with the other remaining 50 percent going to another investor. The plan exceeded everyone's expectations, and even minority shareholder Glenn became a millionaire.

A PERIOD OF PERSONAL EXPLORATION

Affluence could not protect Glenn from the losses of middle age. In addition to his change of career, his accident, and his children growing up, he had aging parents. In February 1966 his father, John Herschel Glenn Sr., who had been taking treatments for prostate cancer, died at home in New Concord. Glenn's mother, Clara Sproat Glenn, died in March 1971 and his father-in-law died that same year.

On January 21, 1967, Glenn and Robert F. Kennedy, with whom the astronaut had renewed a friendship after Herschel Glenn's death, were forced to reevaluate their feelings about the space program. That day, astronauts Gus Grissom, Edward H. White, and Roger Chaffee were the first casualties of Project Apollo. Their deaths in a flash fire on the launch pad highlighted the continuing risks posed by space travel.

Despite the tragedy, both Glenn and Kennedy continued to support space ex-

ploration. To help dispel the cloud left by the disaster, Glenn narrated two TV documentaries designed to justify the Apollo flights. In the first, *Great Explorations*, Glenn drew a comparison between the goals of Moon explorations and the goals of earlier explorers. In the second, *Here Comes Tomorrow*, Glenn discussed passenger travel in space.

Glenn and Kennedy further cemented their friendship when, in 1968, Kennedy decided to campaign for the presidency. Glenn joined him on his campaign tour. Kennedy hoped that Glenn's ties to the military might neutralize the political effect of his opposition to President Johnson's policy in Vietnam, where five hundred thousand American troops were deployed. Kennedy took Glenn along to meetings with leaders of the Black Panthers and on trips through poor ghettos, giving him a taste of what it meant to champion the cause of people caught in poverty.

The Kennedy-Glenn partnership was cut short, however, at the Ambassador Hotel in Los Angeles, California, on June 4, 1968, when Sirhan Sirhan shot and killed Kennedy. Glenn was there and went with the ambulance to the hospital. Ethel, Kennedy's wife, asked Glenn and Annie to stay with the Kennedy children, and it fell to Glenn to tell the children that their father had been assassinated.

In the political aftermath of the tragedy, Glenn took up two of Kennedy's causes. He accepted the chairmanship of the bipartisan Emergency Committee for Gun Control and testified before a Senate sub-

THE GRIEFS OF THE GLENNS

In Famous in America, *Peter N. Carroll discusses the losses sustained by John Glenn in his mid life:*

"Just after Glenn's forty-fifth birthday he began to experience the painful losses of middle age. John Glenn, Sr., member of the Masons, Odd Fellows, and the American Legion, died of cancer in New Concord at the age of seventy-one. A fiery explosion at Cape Kennedy took the lives of astronauts Gus Grissom, Ed White, and Roger Chaffee. On a bright, frosty February morning at Arlington National Cemetery, a stony-faced Glenn helped carry Grissom's flag-draped coffin as tears ran down his face. The next month, he mourned the loss of another pioneer, the Soviet cosmonaut Yuri Gagarin, killed in a plane crash. 'Man tries something, and sometimes he succeeds and sometimes he fails,' said Glenn in a speech to the National Space Club on the fifth anniversary of his flight. 'We hate to lose good friends, but we think that they went in a good cause.' He scoffed at the idea of 'some great cosmic drag race' with the Soviet Union. 'The really important part of the manned space program is exploration in the greatest sense of the word.'"

John Glenn was greatly affected by the deaths of fellow astronauts Gus Grissom, Ed White, and Roger Chaffee pictured here from left to right.

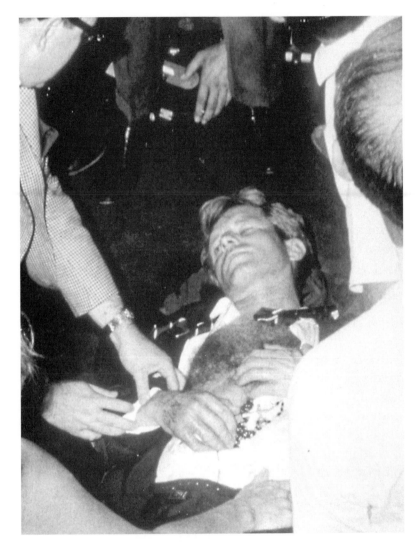

Senator Robert Kennedy lies mortally wounded after being shot in Los Angeles in 1968. John Glenn was in Los Angeles when the assassination occurred and he deeply grieved the death of his friend.

committee. He also became a trustee of the Robert F. Kennedy Foundation (later renamed the Robert F. Kennedy Memorial), which helps the oppressed and disadvantaged and works with AmeriCorps's National Youth Project for young people in neglected neighborhoods.

Kennedy's death also had a personal impact on Glenn. He and Annie became frequent visitors to the Kennedy home. On one of those visits, Glenn came across the essay "Heroism" by Ralph Waldo Emerson. Kennedy had underlined the passage, "If you would serve your brother, because it is fit for you to serve him, do not take back your words when you find that prudent people do not commend you."[70] Remembering Kennedy's courage and willingness to champion those less fortunate than himself, motivated Glenn to take another look at political life.

A Short Return to Political Ambitions

Less than two years later, a political opportunity arose when Ohio senator Stephen Young announced his retirement. Immediately, Glenn indicated his intention to run for Young's Senate seat. "With Young out of the way," says Van Riper, "[Glenn] thought the Democratic nomination would be his for the asking. Glenn still had not shed the naive concept that heroism entitled him to public office. That many other Ohio Democratic politicians seemed to agree only set Glenn up for the difficulties that lay ahead."[71]

His challenger for the 1970 senate nomination was Howard Metzenbaum, a lawyer and ten-year state legislator who had been Young's campaign manager. Although Metzenbaum, an antimilitary Democrat, was relatively unknown in the state of Ohio, he knew his district well, and his ability to raise funds made him a favorite of the Ohio Democratic organization.

Glenn, still sure of his name recognition from his Mercury days, nevertheless protested that he "wasn't running as the first American to orbit the Earth."[72] He tried hard to keep a political focus during campaign rallies, where, he said, "some little kid in the front row would always ask, 'Mr. Glenn, do astronauts really drink Tang [an orange drink]?'"[73]

Glenn's overconfidence about name recognition and his fund-raising experience gave Metzenbaum a clear advantage. As the contest between them developed, Van Riper says,

Metzenbaum organized hard and widely; the estimated $700,000 he spent on the primary attracted attention even from national news magazines. Metzenbaum opened 15 offices around the state with more than 50 paid coordinators. . . . Soon, Glenn, finding himself suddenly surrounded by Metzenbaum advertising and campaign literature, began complaining that Metzenbaum was trying to "buy the election with a million dollars' worth of television spots."[74]

The outcome of the election was predictable to many who observed the differences between the two campaigns. Glenn, discounting his opponent's strength, neglected to build an organization. He preferred appearances in high-school civics classes to meetings with Democratic leaders. Admitting an aversion to raising money, he told Van Riper, "I'd rather wrestle a gorilla."[75] Glenn carried seventy-six Ohio counties—the rural ones. Metzenbaum won in twelve counties—the populous ones. The count made all the difference: Glenn lost the election by thirteen thousand votes.

It was a valuable experience, however. Without learning to like the drudgery of politics, Van Riper writes, Glenn did learn its value:

The primary defeat left Glenn a loser, but a wiser one. Glenn had finally learned that politics was not the simple extension of hero worship. It had its own rules and—not unlike the military—its own traditions which had to be understood, and manipulated, if one were to succeed. Rather than give up after two failed efforts to gain a Senate seat, Glenn decided it was time for the astronaut to become a real politician.[76]

Glenn swallowed his disappointment and pledged to support Metzenbaum, but he had developed an enduring dislike for his fellow Democrat. Throughout the summer, Glenn campaigned actively for John Gilligan, the Democratic candidate for governor of Ohio. In that contest, at least, Glenn proved his value to the Democratic Party. Gilligan won the general election of 1970. Metzenbaum lost, though by a narrow margin, to the Republican candidate.

GAINING A POLITICAL IMAGE

During the next four years Glenn sought out political opportunities. He made innumerable speeches on college campuses. He worked with the staff at the Democratic Party headquarters. He courted a relationship with the party organization and kept his eye on the Senate seat held by Republican William Saxbe, who would be running for reelection in 1974.

In 1973 a chance event changed what some had seen as an obstacle in Glenn's political life. A *Today* show presentation on stuttering convinced Annie to try a new treatment program at Hollins College in Roanoke, Virginia. After only three weeks

John Glenn and his wife, Annie. When Annie conquered her stuttering, she became a confident speaker and more active in Glenn's political campaign.

Annie had retrained her speech muscles to the point of making a phone call without a pause. "Our lives were transformed," says Glenn. "People had always mistaken her reluctance to speak for shyness, but she loved people and was no wallflower."[77] More importantly, her new confidence made her more open to taking a public role.

The opportunity for Annie to enter active campaigning came that same year. Saxbe's Senate seat opened in 1973, when President Nixon appointed Saxbe attorney general. Ohio's Governor Gilligan then appointed Metzenbaum to finish Saxbe's term. This meant that, for Glenn to win a seat in the Senate, he would once again have to campaign against his 1970 challenger. Also, he would have to take on the Ohio Democratic organization, for the top Democrats of Ohio immediately came out for Metzenbaum.

In anticipation of the fight ahead, Glenn resigned from his lucrative position at Royal Crown. Although he still was not thrilled about asking for campaign funds, he entered the political arena again. Media consultant Scott Miller told *People* magazine interviewers that "[Glenn] would come to a fund raiser and stand in a corner talking to Annie or a Secret Service guy, rather than going through the room begging people he didn't particularly respect for money."[78]

Money, however, would once again be a strong indicator. Glenn's second campaign against Metzenbaum became the highest-priced primary race in Ohio's history. Helped by an eighty-thousand-dollar con-tribution from Steve Kovacik, a Columbus attorney, Glenn planned to spend even more than Metzenbaum had spent in 1970. Glenn articulated a high-minded approach to money, reminding the electorate that he could have been a millionaire several times over after his spaceflight but chose to serve his country by seeking public office.

In a carefully calculated campaign, Kovacik, a politically savvy lawyer, helped Glenn specifically in the thickly populated counties where Metzenbaum had done well in 1970. In an interview with the political analyst Richard F. Fenno Jr., an observer explained that

> Steve Kovacik was an ethnic [eastern European] who took John into Northeast Ohio, into the ethnic communities there and got him their support in 1974. John never had problems in Southern Ohio. His problems were in Northeast Ohio, especially Cuyahoga County. Kovacik taught the farm boy how to politick [engage in political activity or discussion] on the ethnic west side of Cleveland. He got John elected in 1974.[79]

In the final exchange of the campaign, Glenn appealed to the patriotism of his voters in a pointed reply to an attack Metzenbaum had made two weeks before the election. Metzenbaum had claimed that Glenn had never held a job. "What followed," said Van Riper, "made Ohio, and possibly national, political history."[80]

Glenn's speechwriters worked hard on their response, then held their fire until a debate the Friday before the primary

WHO IS JOHN GLENN?

In Glenn: The
Astronaut Who
Would Be President,
*Frank Van Riper
discusses the liberal and
conservative sides of
Glenn's character as he
sought the 1984
presidential
nomination.*

"That is the paradox of John Glenn. It is as if there are two John Glenns, each struggling against the other in the public perception. One is the obvious John Glenn, the righteous-living man of unimpeachable morality, a military hero in two wars, an astronaut, patriot and ostensibly a conservative or middle-of-the-roader, in whose hands the government would be secure against all enemies, domestic or foreign. As one political observer portrayed this Glenn, 'He's Ike [President Eisenhower] in a spacesuit.'

But there is another, less advertised but just as real John Glenn. It is the liberal Democratic senator from Ohio whose support of ERA [Equal Rights Amendment], organized labor, civil rights and abortion seems somehow out of character.

In this paradox, Glenn's personality seems to have facets that conflict with the popular image. One might expect the stubbornness that Glenn often displays in public and private life. But equally powerful within Glenn's make-up is a personal sensitivity that can bring him to tears and a tenderness to friends. As a husband, Glenn has spent 41 years married to a woman whose 85% disability stutter—until she was cured five years ago—never caused him embarrassment and often found him on the phone ordering groceries in her place. . . .

As a retired Marine colonel, one would expect Glenn to have a strong 'military' view of world affairs. Glenn does fulfill that image with his support of the B-1 bomber and nerve gas, both of which he believes essential to the nation's safety. But as someone who says 'I know the horrible side of war,' Glenn has confounded his conservative supports by his backing of the nuclear freeze and opposition to much of Reagan's foreign policy in Central America, which he regards as potentially dangerous."

election. Before a sharply divided audience, Glenn directly addressed the issue of his marine record:

> Howard, I can't believe you said that [I never held a job]. . . . You go with me to any gold star mother [women whose sons or daughters were killed in action], and you look her in the eye and tell her that her son did not hold a job.
>
> You go with me to the space program, and you go as I have gone to the widows and orphans of [astronauts] Ed White and Gus Grissom and Roger Chaffee, and you look those kids in the eye and tell them their dad didn't hold a job.
>
> You go with me on Memorial Day . . . and you stand in Arlington National Cemetery—where I have more friends than I like to remember— and you watch those waving flags and you stand there and you think about this nation and you tell me that those people didn't have a job.
>
> I tell you, Howard Metzenbaum, you should be on your knees every day of your life thanking God that there are some men—some men—who held a job. . . .
>
> I've held a job, Howard.[81]

Glenn received a standing ovation and clinched the Ohio Democratic Party nomination for U.S. Senator. His speech set the tone for the remainder of the campaign. In the primary he beat Metzenbaum by a landslide margin of 95,000. In November's general election he beat Ralph J. Perk, the Republican candidate, by more than 1 million votes.

6 The Public Service Politician

John Glenn's career as a U.S. senator began in January 1975 and seemed to promise the same kind of prominence as his military career. He obtained positions on the two committees he asked for—Government Services and Foreign Relations. These two committees were well suited to his scientific expertise, and he worked hard for them. With Mike Mansfield, the Senate majority leader from Montana, as his mentor, Glenn obtained an impressive number of amendments in floor votes.

Among the causes he supported were campaign reform, funding of medical research and education, the right to abortion, and consumer protection. He came out in favor of the Equal Rights Amendment and the Health Education and Welfare Department's effort to ensure equal rights to women in physical education programs.

The 1976 Democratic Convention

It was a sign of his growing stature in the Democratic Party that Glenn was chosen to give the keynote address in Madison Square Garden at the July 1976 Democratic Convention. And he was rumored, along with Walter Mondale and Edmund Muskie, to be a candidate for the running mate of Democratic presidential candidate Jimmy Carter.

The address did not, however, bring Glenn the support he had expected. In fact it did just the opposite. The crowd that had gathered in Madison Square Garden was noisy and unresponsive. Television cameras and monitors focused primarily on people who were not listening to Glenn's words. Two days into the convention, Glenn was still waiting for Carter to make his vice-presidential choice. When the telephone call finally came, Carter said he had picked Walter Mondale.

The Foreign Relations Committee

Disappointed but characteristically resilient, Glenn rededicated himself to the Foreign Relations Committee. In September 1976 he accompanied Senator Mans-

Jimmy Carter and John Glenn stand together on the podium at the 1976 Democratic Convention.

field on a fact-finding trip to China, in the hopes of reestablishing diplomatic relations with the Communist nation. Glenn was able to visit a medical center to discuss Chinese-Taiwanese relations and to fly a Chinese military plane. He concluded that in this country of "vast and complex energies and ambitions"[82] reliance on Western education would prove to be the area of common ground.

In other work with the Foreign Relations Committee, Glenn supported Carter's effort to reduce stockpiles of nuclear weapons. "I thought," Glenn says, "we could promise cooperation in developing peaceful uses of nuclear energy, while using trade and economic sanctions to prevent the spread of weapons."[83] His work, in part, led to the Nuclear Non-Proliferation Act of 1978, the goal of which was to stop the spread of nuclear weapons worldwide. Proud of his contribution, Glenn points to that act as an influential piece of U.S. nuclear policy, noting in his memoir that the provisions of the 1978 law ". . . remain cornerstones of our nuclear foreign policy."[84]

THE GOVERNMENT SERVICES COMMITTEE

In addition to his Foreign Relations Committee work, Glenn served on the Government Services Committee. From 1978 to

1980, work for that committee involved Glenn in negotiations for oil from the Middle East. He joined a congressional delegation hoping to learn how Arab-Israeli conflicts threatened U.S. oil supplies. Glenn and other congressmen met leaders of Israel, Jordan, Saudi Arabia, and other oil-producing countries, as well as of the Palestine Liberation Organization, contributing important insights into the beginnings of a peace agreement. The Camp David Accords, which Israel, the United States, and Egypt eventually signed in September 1978, established a framework for peace in

GLENN'S RESILIENCE IN DISAPPOINTMENT

Commenting on Glenn's keynote address at Madison Square Garden in 1976, Frank Van Riper, in Glenn: The Astronaut Who Would Be President, *discusses the theory that delegates in favor of Mondale had planned to disrupt the speech. Here, he gives the contrasting opinions of one of Glenn's friends, retired lieutenant general Tom Miller, and Robert Strauss, chairman of the Democratic Party.*

"Tom Miller . . . believes the evidence of a plot against Glenn is strong. 'I tell you I saw politics at its worse,' Miller recalls. 'First you got to know that Hubert Humphrey wanted Mondale to be vice-president—there wasn't any doubt about it. John starts speaking, he's about five or ten minutes into the meat of what he was trying to say, and Humphrey comes on the floor, enters the door almost directly under the podium.'

'The press forgot all about Glenn and went roaring over to [Humphrey]. There must have been 50 people rushing to him. Now how much more can you disrupt a speaker? Then he holds that little press conference. Then just as that's beginning to break up, who enters the floor but the congressman from New Jersey, Peter Rodino. It was just so carefully orchestrated.'

Robert Strauss refutes the charge. 'Ridiculous,' he says. 'I knew every . . . thing that was going on in that hall. If there had been any plot against Glenn, I would have known about it. I had people all over there doing nothing but watching just for that sort of thing. There was no point in being paranoid about it. Glenn simply gave a speech that was not well written.'

'America liked him in spite of the speech,' Strauss says. 'We polled after it, and the ones who saw it on television liked him. The press just decided to paste [strike hard at] him like hell and they did.'"

the Middle East and were, to Glenn and the rest of America, a great success.

However, Glenn was not convinced that the twenty years allowed by the Camp David negotiations would be enough security for U.S. oil needs. With characteristic thoroughness and concern, he reviewed the mission of the Department of Energy (DOE), which strategized the nation's transition from a dependency on oil to other sources of energy. Following this review, he began to study how to switch the nation from dependence on oil to more diversified sources of energy.

Glenn suspected that nuclear energy might be a solution, but that possibility was called into question in 1979, following a near meltdown at the Three Mile Island nuclear power plant in southeastern Pennsylvania. The consequent release of radiation caused a public outcry against the use of nuclear power for any purpose. At issue was not only the danger of meltdown but the amount of radiation routinely received by workers on the job. It was a concern to which Glenn continued to search for a solution.

The next year he recommended a higher budget for the DOE in order to give the department "sufficient resources to accomplish . . . energy research and development."[85] His recommendation of $601,682,000 would fund research on coal and coal-derived synthetics, solar technologies, oil shale, and unconventional gas supplies over the next five years. Beyond the twenty-year limit of the Camp David Accords, he hoped that renewable energy sources and advanced nuclear technologies would begin to fulfill the nation's needs.

Glenn also continued work on behalf of the workers at risk for radiation. On October 7, 1981, his committee asked the General Accounting Office (GAO) to fund needed research into problems with radiation exposure in the nuclear energy industry. The report, which was sent to Glenn by the GAO not quite a year later, revealed that, "from 1969 to 1980, the number of workers exposed per reactor has increased approximately eightfold. [And] the collective dose [of radiation—that is, the total dose received by all nuclear power plant workers] has increased substantially."[86] With Glenn's active encouragement, both federal agencies and the nuclear industry developed and implemented efforts to reduce the risk of on-the-job exposure to radiation.

THE SALT II TREATY

The Nuclear Non-Proliferation Act turned out to be only the beginning of the increasingly complex issues brought before Glenn and the Foreign Relations Committee. As the United States sought to stop the spread of nuclear weapons, government officials hoped to involve the Soviet Union in the process. The Strategic Arms Limitation Treaty (SALT II) was one result of this international diplomacy. SALT II was a treaty between the United States and Soviet Union that reduced the number of launchers capable of carrying warheads. To Glenn, the Foreign Relations Committee's work on SALT II seemed, at first, "an avenue for pursuing peace."[87]

However, when revolution erupted in Iran, jeopardizing two verification stations set up there to monitor the Soviet's activities, SALT II suddenly seemed to have insufficient safeguards. Many in the United States, including Glenn, believed that the Soviets were not trustworthy. If U.S. officials could not monitor the Communist nation's activities, Glenn was unwilling to support a treaty that demanded cooperation from both sides. Although he agreed with President Carter's hope for quick disarmament, he clashed with the president by insisting that the treaty needed stricter requirements to verify that the Soviet Union was complying.

After becoming part of a special delegation to the Soviet Union in November 1978 to discuss SALT II, Glenn returned even more firmly convinced that strict verification was an absolute necessity. In Senate deliberations on SALT II he argued successfully for his position and won stricter verification amendments.

His success in the Senate, though, strained his relationship with Carter and the treaty stalled in the Foreign Relations Committee. However, before the differences were resolved, the Soviet Union invaded Afghanistan, a move that changed Carter's stand and proved Glenn's point. As Carroll writes, "Glenn's opposition to Carter did not end until the president changed his foreign policy. . . . Feeling betrayed by the Soviet invasion of Afghanistan, Carter gained Glenn's support by rekindling the cold war. In January 1980 the president asked for a postponement of the vote on SALT II."[88]

Following Carter's switch in policy, Glenn made a decision that brought him back into the public eye. He endorsed Carter for a second term as president. In fact, his support was largely responsible for Carter's win in the Ohio primary and was a deciding factor in his nomination.

Simultaneously, Glenn ran his own reelection campaign, and the Ohio voters returned him to the Senate by an overwhelming majority of 1.6 million (69 percent of the total vote). Although Carter went on to lose to Ronald Reagan in the national election, the active campaigning had made Glenn more visible. Coupled with his leadership on the nuclear weapons treaty, the new confidence and poise that Glenn showed in the political arena opened up a new possibility: People began to ask if he were considering a higher public office, namely the U.S. presidency.

A REAGAN DEMOCRAT

Meanwhile, Reagan's 1980 election signaled the return of a conservative political climate. The conservativism, Glenn explained, was a result of the creation of a new social class: "We have created a great new middle class of people with better incomes, better homes, and better opportunities for their kids. These people are now concerned that they not regress—a fear that has created perhaps a whole new wave toward traditional Republicanism."[89]

Glenn's explanation indicated that he was becoming more willing to adopt a political image. As a Democratic senator, he had opposed his own party's president.

Following the Soviet invasion of Afghanistan and a resulting change in U.S. foreign policy, President Carter regained Glenn's support.

Now, with a Republican in the White House, Glenn had to find a way to reconcile his liberal and conservative leanings.

Glenn began to recognize that he had many conservative-sounding approaches to the issues of the Reagan administration. After his 1980 reelection, Glenn's views were so similar to the new president's that the issues they addressed were often the same: the balanced budget, the need to stimulate productivity, and the importance of private enterprise. In other words, Glenn often talked like a Republican, making comments such as, "We can't interfere,

by too much taxation and regulation, with business's ability to be competitive."[90]

Glenn supported Reagan's new economic program, called Reaganomics, which focused mainly on instituting massive tax cuts. Because Glenn refused to oppose policies he agreed with simply on the basis of party affiliation, his support of Reaganomics was the first step in establishing himself as a political moderate. He saw himself going above and beyond the party organization and appealing to the public at large. In his winning 1980 senate reelection campaign, for example, he had

not needed the Democratic Party. On his credentials as a good senator alone, he had run and had won as a middle-of-the-road politician, unwilling to limit his ideas with a political party philosophy. Glenn said, "I'm a hard fish to hold down. . . . I don't like the idea of being pigeon-holed into one ideological mold, then have people think I'm going to have a knee-jerk reaction in response to their pressure. . . . I never give it a thought whether [my vote] is going to be looked at as liberal or conservative."[91]

THINKING ABOUT THE PRESIDENCY

On April 3, 1981, Glenn took his non-partisan philosophy to Jackson, Mississippi, to give a speech at the Democrats' Jefferson-Jackson Day dinner. This pre-campaign pep talk was the first step on the road to the 1984 presidential election. Reporters began comparing him with other possible presidential candidates, including Ted Kennedy and Walter Mondale.

GLENN ANNOUNCES HIS CANDIDACY FOR PRESIDENT

On April 21, 1983, Frank Van Riper watched the television announcement in which Glenn said he was ready to lead the nation. He recalls that moment in his book Glenn: The Astronaut Who Would Be President.

"In the cool medium of television, Glenn appeared forceful, able—even eloquent—as he reminisced to his audience about his small-town origins, the epic space ride, then pronounced himself ready to lead the nation:

'Today, as I stand at the threshold of an even greater journey,' Glenn said, 'my feelings are the same. I seek your support and God's guidance as once more I ask to serve.'

'With confidence that my life has prepared me, with dedication to the promise of opportunity and the pursuit of peace, and with a firm belief that guided by the light of old values we can again reach new horizons, I declare my candidacy for president of the United States.'

It had taken 21 years since his historic flight in space to convince millions that an astronaut could be seriously considered as a national politician. But now the press and public seemed willing to accept John Glenn not only as a great American hero but as a true candidate for the presidency."

Glenn's political skills were becoming stronger. On May 14, 1981, he gave the keynote address at the Cook County Democratic Party dinner in Chicago. For this event, the Ohio press was on hand and afterward rated Glenn's speech as an improvement over the uninspiring delivery that had, so far, been his trademark.

It took more than two successful speeches, however, for Glenn to become a viable presidential candidate. Until late in 1982, says Washington political analyst Richard F. Fenno Jr., Glenn's responses to reporters were that he was only "thinking very seriously" about it, or "keeping the options open."[92] At the same time, says Fenno, after the April trip to Mississippi, Glenn began experimenting with the idea of a presidential campaign. He was asking himself if he could win, what it would cost him (monetarily and personally), how he should try to present himself, and who would support him. For Glenn, the question of support deeply involved Annie. She was reluctant, so Glenn would say only that he had come to no decision.

Nonetheless, as the campaign progressed, Glenn began to see himself as separate from the two most prominent Democratic hopefuls, Mondale and Kennedy. During 1982 Mondale gave 150 speeches in thirty-eight states and began courting the endorsement of the labor movement. To Glenn, these moves were both premature and counterproductive.

Even though Kennedy's precampaign ideas often paralleled Glenn's, especially in regard to public service, Glenn's previous connections with the Kennedys made him reluctant to run against a member of that family. Only after Kennedy dropped out of the presidential campaign in October 1982 did Glenn seriously consider becoming a candidate. Glenn writes,

> To that point, the media had played up the head-to-head conflict between Kennedy and Mondale. . . . So when Kennedy dropped out, . . . It became Mondale and Glenn. At that point, I had to decide whether or not I thought the direction Reagan was leading the country was the right direction. I decided it was not. I did not like the turn the economy was taking, the drift of foreign policy, policies in areas like civil rights, the elderly, environmental enforcement. So I decided to run.[93]

Another major factor that led to Glenn's decision to campaign for the presidency was that Annie had finally softened to the idea. As Glenn recalls,

> [Annie] and I had talked all of this out. She had continued to improve her speaking, returning to Hollins for a second round of training and, most recently, working regularly with a speech therapist at the Walter Reed Army Medical Center in Washington. She also had spoken for the first time to a large audience, three hundred women in Canton, Ohio. Annie, who once would have been petrified at speaking to a crowd a tenth that size, told the story of her difficulties, fears, and humiliations as a stutterer. It was another first for our family, the first

full-length speech she had ever given, and it reduced her audience to tears. I knew she was brave, dedicated, and determined. But we had both been around politics long enough to know how brutal a campaign could be. I needed to know if she was up to it. She told me she was game.[94]

A Presidential Candidate

The spring of 1983 found Glenn moving with considerable momentum into a successful campaign. After hiring the humorist Art Buchwald as a speechwriter, he scored a hit on March 26 at the Gridiron Club, a powerful organization of

As John Glenn became more involved in politics he hired humorist Art Buchwald (pictured here) as his speechwriter.

journalists. Glenn delivered the speech well, and the journalists gave him good reviews. On April 21, 1983, he made his formal announcement of entry into the race. By May the national polls gave him an 80 percent approval rating over Mondale's 69 percent.

Glenn's vision included both domestic and foreign policy. On the home front, he envisioned a national service program for youths or the unemployed and national health care. Regarding foreign relations, he cited the experience he had gained working with the Foreign Relations Committee. As an expert in military affairs, he spoke out on national defense, criticizing the development of the stealth bomber (he thought it would be outdated too soon), and calling for renewed efforts for negotiations between Israel and the Palestine Liberation Organization.

Following his well-received speech at the Gridiron Club, Glenn began to speak out against Reagan. Unlike the president, Glenn proposed new, pragmatic programs for improving the economy and an end to the arms race. His and Reagan's ideas contrasted most strongly in regard to Central America. Glenn writes,

> My military background would counter Reagan's strident anti-Communism, which had led him to treat the Marxist [Communist] Sandinista regime in Nicaragua as a major threat to democracy in Central America. I opposed funding the anti-Sandinista contras, on the grounds that they were little more than surrogates for the right-wing landowners who had held sway [were influential] in the country for years. Although the Sandinistas were encouraging an insurgency [revolt] in El Salvador, I didn't consider them much of a threat.[95]

By the middle of 1983, Glenn's chances of winning looked good. His record, combined with his ruminations, seemed to foreshadow a presidency with a mandate from the people and a charismatic moderation. According to biographer Frank Van Riper, Glenn would, if elected, have "one of the most surprising [administrations] in American history."[96]

UNSHAKABLE CONFIDENCE

By the time Glenn made a formal announcement of his candidacy, he was fairly confident that he could run a winning campaign. A year and a half before the national election, a late start by presidential campaign standards, Glenn felt he was a strong candidate and a formidable opponent to fellow Democratic senator Walter Mondale.

Glenn's confidence seemed warranted because he had easily won his bid for reelection to the Senate. Furthermore, his financial decisions and investments had made him a wealthy man. So confident was he that he did not start fund-raising until September 1983, nearly six months after his announcement. He had not wanted to do it at all, so his fund-raising efforts lagged behind all of the other candidates.

The Greatest Good for the Most People

In The Presidential Odyssey of John Glenn, *political analyst Richard F. Fenno Jr. quotes Glenn on the importance of maintaining balance in government.*

"The art of government is the balance that we have to set, back and forth between conflicting interests. To produce jobs, you have to have investment. To have investment and having people put their hard-earned savings into investment you need good management. So there's a balance here between investment and management and labor's interest back and forth. You can't go all to labor and you can't go all the other way to business either. We set these balances in our society and that's what we have to take into account. That's what it means to be out in the middle of the political spectrum. It means you're considering these balances that keep our nation going on what is the greatest good for the greatest number of people.

We could tell you right now that we are going to set environmental laws that are going to be the best, that we are going to make the cleanest environment, and we are not going to have any problems whatsoever for the future. We could put them into effect tomorrow morning, and what would we do? We would probably put 10 million people out of work, too. And so there is that kind of a balance back and forth, too. On the other hand, you can't say, 'OK, we are going to create so many jobs we'll take all the scrubbers off the smokestacks, we're not going to worry about pesticides, we don't care if we do pollute, we don't care if there's toxic waste, we've got to provide jobs.' And that would be foolish, too. Because once again, we're unbalancing things in one direction or another.

That's what government's all about. And that's what's hard to sell in a candidacy where you're trying to consider these things and not overpromise and not just go before every group and say, 'Yeah, I'm for you. I'm for whatever it is you want. I promise you.' Because all that winds up with is a presidency where you have overpromised and you can't possibly perform and keep the balances that the president of the United States has to keep—that's in the greatest interest of the greatest number of people."

Glenn also was confident that his name was sufficiently recognizable without campaign publicity. In addition, his publicity staff was delighted about an astronaut movie whose release coincided with the campaign. *The Right Stuff*, a film adaptation of Tom Wolfe's 1979 book about Project Mercury, was coming out in the fall of 1983. As Fenno says, "[Glenn] believed that because of his head start in favorable name recognition, he could afford to wait longer than normal before committing himself to the race. . . . This idea, that he needed only fourteen to sixteen months of full-scale effort became a fixed star in his strategic reckoning."[97]

Reporters, however, saw the possibility of the film having negative effects. *Newsweek*'s Tom Morganthau, Richard Manning, and Howard Fineman, for example, thought the film might complicate Glenn's attempt to rise beyond out of the astronaut image. They cautioned that "the larger question, all sides agree, is whether the cinematic heroics will convince anybody that Glenn deserves to be president."[98]

Glenn himself did deeply desire to be recognized as a presidential candidate rather than as an astronaut. He took pleasure in incidents when that happened, such as at a live broadcast press conference with host Martin Kalb: "When we

Glenn's vote on October 28, 1981 in favor of selling F-15s (shown here) to Saudi Arabia jeopardized Glenn's support from some special interest groups during the 1984 presidential campaign.

went on the air . . . the very first question went to foreign policy . . . , and not once did they mention space — some of the nation's most hard-bitten reporters. I have not been trying to dodge the space profession. But I have been trying to win my spurs in another line of endeavor. Nothing could have pleased me more."[99]

THE REAL WORLD OF NOMINATION POLITICS

Nevertheless, for some unaccountable reason, perhaps simply out of habit, Glenn failed to realize that he was not using his advantages. It was only on September 6, 1983, that Glenn made his first effort to play politics by appealing to interest groups.

That day he gave a luncheon speech at the Foreign Policy Association in the hopes of winning the Jewish vote of New York by supporting the Israelis. For a senator who had voted to sell F-15 jets to Saudi Arabia and criticized Israel's raid on the Iraqi nuclear reactor two years earlier, the bid was too little and too late.

New York's Jews were just one group that would not support him. In the end, he was left with no party alliances, much less any support from organized labor, blacks, or women. Thus, his advantages of wealth and prior-to-campaign name recognition were vanishing one by one.

Without vigorous campaigning, the important Iowa caucuses and the New Hampshire primary vote were upon him all too soon. Both Mondale and a third-runner, Senator Gary Hart, were giving their all to these bell-ringer contests. In both states they were speaking to the local voters in a way calculated to win their support. Glenn, by contrast concentrated on the idea that he was the "electable" candidate of the three, the only one who could beat Reagan.

The truth was, Glenn's Senate record of hard work, study, analysis, reports, and legislative effort was unimportant to a public asking, What do you stand for? What are your views? not, What have you done? For Glenn, the election was about who would be the best president, and he was unprepared to go head to head with the other candidates. When Mondale's aides, for example, noted that Glenn was attacking the same 1981 tax cuts he had himself voted for, the Ohio senator had no response and no suggestion for how he would deal with the issue. Compared with Mondale's and Hart's willingness to say what they thought about tax cuts, it was pointless for Glenn to contend that he could beat Reagan in the November election.

In addition, Glenn's image was suffering as a result of two personality traits that had benefited him as a military hero. First, in combat or in orbit, Glenn had always made decisions on his own. In politics, a lingering tendency to be a loner forced him into making decisions without counsel. The lack of second opinions meant he had no correction for mistakes in instinct. Second, his aggressive responses under personal attack, such as had intensified his ability to shoot back in battle, looked different when seen on national television. In that medium, they

Annie's Triumph

All of their lives the Glenns had lived with Annie's struggles with stuttering. In John Glenn: A Memoir, *Glenn tells how interested he and Annie were to hear one night in 1973, on the* Today *show, about a new treatment for stuttering developed by Ron Webster of Hollins College in Roanoke, Virginia.*

"'That's a new approach,' [Glenn] said when the *Today* segment ended. 'It looks good. Do you want to try it?'

Annie was excited at the prospect.

Soon she was enrolled in a three-week course at Hollins that had her and other stutterers working intensively eleven hours a day. The theory behind the exercises was that speech patterns are set to a large degree by audio feedback, sounds and vibrations that let us pick up continuity and rhythm. If the nerve, brain, and muscle combinations that do this had some congenital weakness or for some reason got out of sync during childhood, stuttering could develop. Sometimes the stutterer's hearing could block out information given the brain by the sound of the voice, causing the speech muscles to jump out of control. The goal was to retrain the system and reestablish control.

Students relearned alphabetical sounds from the ground up and spent hours practicing them, then spoke syllables, dragging them out to two seconds, and progressed from there. The final exercise, at the end of the three weeks, had the students doing something Annie had never been able to do before. I'll never forget her phone call.

'John,' she said on the line from Virginia; forming her words slowly and carefully as the muscles worked, 'Today we went to a shopping center and went shopping. And I could ask for things. Imagine that.'

I had never heard Annie speak that many words without a single pause. It was all I could do to reply, 'That's wonderful!'

'I think so, too,' she said slowly. 'It's a start.'"

seemed more like self-preservation reflexes.

STEPPING OUT OF THE RACE

Glenn rated a low third place in both Iowa and New Hampshire. Yet, unwilling or unable to accept the losses, he decided to blitz the voters of Alabama, Georgia, and Florida with political ads. He hoped their Super Tuesday primaries, held on March 13, 1984, would prove that the Iowa and New Hampshire contests were not really indicative of the people's will. The blitz, however, also put Glenn deeply in debt. Most of the $2.8 million he eventually owed was money he spent after he lost in Iowa.

The Super Tuesday primaries were a disaster, and Glenn announced his withdrawal from the presidential race two days later. He admits in his memoir that he should have quit sooner:

> Quitting has always been hard for me, and I gritted my teeth, borrowed money with the support of my strongest backers, and headed into Super Tuesday thinking that I might salvage my candidacy there. It was potentially my strongest area. But the defeats in Iowa and New Hampshire were too much to overcome, and my results in the three vital southern primaries were no better.[100]

Glenn was disappointed because he felt that issues had not decided the election outcome. His bid for the presidency was over, and the winner of the nomination, Walter Mondale, would prove unelectable against Ronald Reagan.

Quietly Glenn finished the last two years of his second Senate term. In a Republican-dominated Senate, he removed himself from the Foreign Relations Committee and chose, instead, the Armed Services Committee, where he thought his expertise had a chance of fruitful service.

NUCLEAR FEARS AT HOME IN OHIO

Soon after Reagan's second inauguration in January 1985, Glenn had an opportunity to redefine his party line, test his leadership, reassess his satisfaction with legislative work in the Senate, and render service to both the armed services and the people who manufactured their weapons. A delegation of citizens from Fernald, Ohio, the Fernald Residents for Environmental Safety and Health visited Glenn's office to complain about safety conditions in the nuclear weapons plant in their town.

Glenn immediately had the Governmental Affairs Committee investigate the nation's nuclear weapons plants. The resulting report, which detailed a history of alarming deterioration in safety procedures, not only in Ohio but also at all seventeen U.S. nuclear weapons plants, prompted Glenn to recommend a monitoring system for all plants. The monitors recorded continuing increases in the radiation levels to which plant employees were exposed, caused by aging of the plants and premature failure of some plant equipment.

The space shuttle Challenger *explodes seconds after launch. The 1986 tragedy brought John Glenn back into the spotlight as he helped NASA and the families of the victims deal with their losses.*

Glenn's report also revealed that cleanup and modernization would cost hundreds of billions of dollars and stretch past the year 2000. As a result, he introduced a bill that reflected the Democrats' approach to the problem. When the bill became law, it established the Nuclear Defense Facility Safety Board. As with Glenn's previous nuclear-related work, he found the success of this legislative initiative very affirming because it represented government serving the citizens.

LEGISLATIVE WORK IN THE AFTERMATH OF TRAGEDY

Glenn's work with the Armed Services Committee also involved him with ongoing NASA projects, one of which was the development of a reusable space shuttle. It was the tragic conclusion of one of those space shuttle projects, *Challenger*, that brought John Glenn back into the spotlight.

On January 28, 1986, many Americans were gathered around television sets and at the Kennedy Space Center on Cape Canaveral to see the *Challenger*'s launch. On board were six astronauts and a civilian, sixth-grade teacher Christa McAuliffe. Seventy-three seconds after liftoff, the shuttle exploded into a gigantic fireball. Already at the space center for the launch, Glenn stayed on, consoling families and analyzing errors.

The week that followed, Fenno says, proved to be "one of John Glenn's finest weeks of national service, and it was wholly dependent on his experience as an astronaut. It also reminded people of the blend of heroism and strength of character that had always been the source of his appeal as a public figure."[101]

Glenn's prominent role after the tragedy had the side effect of assuring him a successful campaign for Senate reelection in 1986. Due to his continuing popularity in Ohio and partly due to a $234,000 campaign contribution from Charles F. Keating, the chief financial officer of Lincoln Savings and Loan in Phoenix, Arizona, Glenn did not go into debt.

It had been fifteen years since John Glenn had orbited Earth in *Friendship 7*. During that time, the years he spent in the Senate reflected a concern for and obligation to the American people. And his foray into presidential politics only deepened his will to accept his share of responsibility for democratic government.

7 Back in Orbit

Glenn's senior status as a third-term senator was a growing source of satisfaction for him. His satisfaction deepened when election results around the country brought to Washington enough new Democrats to make a majority in the Senate. Glenn, therefore, became the chair of the Governmental Affairs Committee and was able to push through legislation designed to reduce government spending, establish mandatory financial officers in many federal agencies, and institute policies to uncover wasteful government practices and identify potential savings.

MORE OIL PROBLEMS IN THE MIDDLE EAST

In early 1987, as the Senate Foreign Relations Committee's focus returned to the Middle East, a review of the Middle East's role in serving U.S. energy needs commandeered several months of Glenn's time. Iranian militants in the war between Iran and Iraq attacked Kuwaiti oil tankers and then fired on the U.S. ship *Stark.* Hoping to avoid a war, Senate majority leader Jim Sasser responded by sending Glenn and Senator John Warner on a trip to visit

friendly Middle Eastern countries, Bahrain, Kuwait, Oman, Qatar, Saudi Arabia, and the United Arab Emirates in the Persian Gulf.

The report that Glenn and Warner submitted on June 17, 1987, stressed the importance of understanding that although these Arab nations were interested in protecting U.S. interests, they did not want to do it by themselves. Instead, they wanted the United States to protect its own interest in Middle Eastern oil by committing U.S. naval ships to accompany the tankers through hostile waters. Glenn was not willing to agree to this though because the Middle East served other Western nations' oil needs as well. He objected, saying that the United States alone should not be militarily responsible for all the Western oil. And he worried, Glenn said, "that only U.S. servicemen might be killed or captured,"[102] a possibility he coud not justify.

As an alternative, Glenn recommended putting pressure on Iran and Iraq to end their war and on England, France, and other nations to stop arms sales to Iran. He hoped better cooperation with the allies would diffuse hostilities. And indeed, by the following year, Iran and Iraq had reached a peace agreement, allowing the tankers to pass the countries unharassed.

A CAMPAIGN CONTRIBUTION BOOMERANGS

In March 1987, while Glenn was deeply involved in the Middle East situation, he heard from one of his 1986 campaign contributors, Charles F. Keating. Keating's lawyer, James Grogan, a former intern in the Senate, contacted Glenn over what seemed like a routine complaint about the Federal Home Loan Bank Board's audit of Lincoln Savings and Loan (S&L) in Phoenix, Arizona. The auditors, Grogan said, usually finished up in about three months, but they had been at the S&L for nearly a year.

Keating had also contacted his Arizona senators, Dennis DeConcini and John McCain, and had asked two other senators in states where he had business interests to meet with Grogan and bank board representative Edwin Gray. Gray, however, said he could not discuss the audit in detail and asked them all to return a week later for a meeting with the bank examiners in question.

At this meeting, on April 9, 1987, the bank board examiners explained that charges were, in fact, pending against Keating's shaky S&L, and that Keating had been in trouble before. "When one of them said their investigation would result in criminal referrals," Glenn later wrote, "I closed my notepad and dropped all involvement with the matter."[103]

The government's Regulatory Trade Commission ultimately sued Keating for

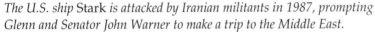

The U.S. ship Stark *is attacked by Iranian militants in 1987, prompting Glenn and Senator John Warner to make a trip to the Middle East.*

John Glenn resented an investigation into his campaign relations with Charles F. Keating (shown here).

cheating Lincoln Savings and Loan and its investors of $1.1 billion. Keating was sentenced to ten years in prison.

Nearly two years later, in 1989, as Congress was allocating $300 billion to bail out Lincoln Savings and Loan, Glenn was asked to account for his relationship with Keating. Republicans in Ohio convinced the Senate that all five senators who had received contributions from the banker should be investigated by the Senate Ethics Committee. The senators became known as the Keating Five, and the inves-

tigation stretched to February 27, 1991. The final report, however, contained only mild reprimands, as no evidence was found to convict the senators of any wrongdoing.

Glenn, who felt his campaign finances were clearly in order, resented the investigation, and his anger confirmed his decision to campaign for a fourth term in the Senate. Throughout his life, Glenn had been most careful about his ethical standards. After such a track record, he says, "there was no way I was going to let an unwarranted inquiry end my commitment to public service."[104] Following a hard and expensive contest, Glenn became the first senator from Ohio to serve four terms.

As part of the Ohio Democratic organization, Glenn's campaign also supported 1992 presidential candidate William Jefferson Clinton for the Democratic Party nomination. In fact, Glenn became crucial to the Clinton campaign in Ohio when he personally convinced Clinton not to withdraw from the key state. Clinton listened, and as Glenn writes in his memoir, "on election night Clinton's victory in Ohio tipped the balance and commentators started declar-

ing him the winner. He thanked me later, in an inscribed photo, for refusing 'to let me [Clinton] give up on Ohio.'"[105]

A FLIGHT-HUNGRY FORMER ASTRONAUT DARES TO HOPE

During Glenn's fourth-term in the Senate, an international space station became both NASA's top priority and its most expensive venture, and he supported the budget requests in Congress. Since the mission would keep scientists and astronauts in space over extended periods,

John Glenn supported William Jefferson Clinton for the Democratic Presidential Nomination in 1992.

many of NASA's research studies, called space medicine, were centered on the medical effects of a prolonged space mission.

In 1995 the space medicine reports that came across Glenn's desk included some gerontological, or aging, research by three NASA doctors. The report, "Space Physiology and Medicine," presented information showing that the wear and tear on the human body during space travel were essentially the same as the natural aging process. Suddenly, being "too old" began to look like an opportunity for John Glenn.

The parallels between space aging and natural aging gave Glenn an idea. He saw space medicine as his ticket back into space. Glenn began to make the rounds at NASA. He went for a friendly, supportive talk with the report's authors, Arnauld Nicogossian, Sam Pool, and Carolyn Huntoon. He began to show up around the Johnson Space Center in visits he connected with the aging studies. He initiated a medical conversation with Dr. Joan Vernikos, the director of the Life Sciences Division of NASA. He also visited his old friend NASA director Dan Goldin. He even found an occasion to mention his conversations with Goldin to President Clinton and to admit his desire to go up again.

CAMPAIGN FINANCING

As Congress reconvened in January 1997, Glenn had to give up any hopes that Clinton might support his project. Amidst charges that the Clinton campaign had illegally accepted funds from a foreign country, the president was hardly in a position to offer help to anyone. Moreover, as the ranking Democratic member of the Governmental Affairs Committee, Glenn himself became deeply involved in studying Clinton's campaign. The situation demanded that he deal with the political issues at hand and put aside his research proposal and space aspirations. However, Glenn never forgot his desire to go into space again. He began formulating a plan of action and started discussing it with Annie. In light of their talks and the fact that if he pursued a fifth Senate term, he would be eighty-three at its end, he took a further step toward another spaceflight. On February 20, 1997, he announced his intention to resign from the Senate at the end of his fourth term.

A LONG ROAD TO SPACE SHUTTLE *DISCOVERY*

Once he publicized his decision to quit the Senate, Glenn took serious steps toward realizing his self-initiated plan to get NASA to launch him into space again. He asked U.S. Navy admiral John Eisold, the attending physician for Congress, for a thorough physical exam and was reassured that he had no physical problems that would preclude spaceflight. Likewise, he made a formal appointment with Dan Goldin to explain his space research on aging.

Glenn knew, of course, as *Life* magazine writer Richard B. Stolley affirms,

John Glenn talked to his old friend Dan Goldin, director of NASA (shown here), when he decided he wanted to become involved in the space program again.

that "NASA set the ground rules: The mission had to make scientific sense to its own doctors. Also, Glenn would have to pass the same rigorous physical exam as the other crew members—'No waivers.'"[106] Glenn cleared these two hurdles by asking the Johnson Space Center to give him all the tests the astronauts were taking. He took his proposal to NASA officials, and they agreed to consider his request.

On the home front, Glenn approached Annie and the family with his idea. Their support was important to him, and he began a serious campaign to win their approval. In 1997, for their traditional Christmas outing, the family (which now included Dave's wife, Karen, and their two sons) vacationed in Vail, Colorado. They exchanged presents and had dinners together. It was during these dinners that Glenn discussed his idea of going back into

"The World's Oldest Astronaut"

Matt Bai, a reporter for Time, *followed Glenn around the Johnson Space Center in Houston, Texas, as he trained for the* Discovery *mission. In his article "The Time Traveler," Bai describes Glenn's willingness and ability to complete whatever tasks NASA officials presented.*

"For Glenn, however, the fun soon gave way to hours spent studying training manuals. He would be a human test subject on Discovery, giving blood and urine, plastering himself with electrodes to measure his heart rate. He would swallow a pill the size of a bottle cap, inside of which was a tiny thermometer and transmitter to gauge his body temperature. He would be learning to sleep, shower and share space in zero gravity for [eight] days. On his first historic flight, 36 years ago, Glenn had been strapped into the Friendship 7 capsule alone, barely able to move, much less float around. When it came to flying the shuttle—the most complicated vehicle ever built, with more than 800 control switches, 2,600 cargo items, 83 scientific experiments and a satellite on board—the old man had a lot to learn.

So began the re-education of the world's oldest astronaut for his final mission. . . . At times exhausted by 12-hour days in the classrooms and simulators at Johnson [Space Center], Glenn seemed like a grandfather trying to program his VCR. 'Yup . . . yup . . . yup.' he repeated, squinting through glasses and nodding slowly. But NASA's crack instructors soon found out what anyone who knew the longtime senator could have told them: Glenn doesn't always get things right the first time, but he's simply unable to give up. Day after day, he attacked the most tedious assignments—learning to use a 70-mm camera or a blood centrifuge—for hours on end without a hint of frustration. This was the John Glenn from the Mercury days, the 'clean Marine' who ran laps at Langley Air Force Base while his fellow astronauts slept in. After all these years, he was still the John Glenn of American lore—the Midwestern hero who convinced us, through doggedness and decency, that American ingenuity would ultimately win the day."

space. He hoped the details of his proposed NASA mission would win them over. To his disappointment, they departed without giving him any wholehearted assurances.

Three weeks later, on January 15, 1998, came the long-awaited call from Goldin at NASA. Glenn could plan on the launch. Goldin told him, "You're the most persistent man I've ever met. You've passed all your physicals, the science is good, and we've called a news conference tomorrow to announce that John Glenn's going back into space."[107]

After he got the official go-ahead, Glenn's family neither applauded nor stood in his way. It was not until a full two weeks after the press conference that he began to realize how far Annie and the family were from sharing his excitement. At a celebration of the coming launch, Glenn introduced his son to Goldin. Goldin, in turn, remarked that Dave must be excited about his father's flight. "Actually no," Dave answered. "I'm totally against it."[108] And to *Newsweek* writer Matt Bai, Glenn's daughter, Lyn said, "Do I want him to do it? No. . . . Would I ask him not to do it? Never. This is who he is."[109]

Not surprisingly, the announcement of Glenn's voyage, coming soon after his defense of President Clinton's campaign-funding practices, raised some eyebrows. Reporters asked if the trip were a payoff, if NASA had really wanted the research,

Glenn (back row, far right) with fellow Discovery *crew members.*

if Glenn's willingness to be a guinea pig would really provide useful scientific data, and if his hero status warranted all of this attention. To some, the trip was reckless; to others it was worthless. To John Glenn, though, it was necessary.

A Research Assignment

The two-year buildup to Glenn's return to space was based on his conviction that gerontological research was needed in a society whose median age was increasing dramatically. His research, he argued, would help older people adjust to changing conditions such as the loss of bone density. Seniors also could benefit from knowing how muscle tissue reacts to stress. Knowing how muscles react in weightlessness, where they have no exertion against the ordinary force of gravity, could help seniors develop exercise programs.

One of the most important studies that Glenn would be involved in was a heart test. Often when astronauts returned from space, they felt faint after standing still for a few minutes. The *Newsweek* article "Exploring the Secrets of Age" explains that in space the astronauts' hearts "send an oversupply of blood to the head, causing a swollen face and a stuffy nose. As the body adjusts, its total fluid volume declines by as much as a liter, and the entire cardiovascular system relaxes, gradually weakening the heart muscle itself."[110] Glenn's study would compare older and younger people's reactions to this loss of the heart's ordinary need to send blood to the head against the pull of gravity.

Only One John Glenn

Equally important to the scientific research was the proof that even a seventy-seven-year-old senator could successfully undergo the grueling reeducation necessary for the *Discovery* trip. Without a hint of frustration, Glenn managed his legislative duties while attending to his training process. Quiet and self-effacing, he also went about becoming acquainted with the *Discovery* crew, which included the first Japanese woman in space, Chiaki Mukai. And he was patient with dozens of reporters who besieged him everywhere. "So many [NASA] staffers wanted to wish him luck," writes Matt Bai, "that he could hardly find time to eat."[111]

One of the greatest achievements of his *Discovery* flight, however, was that the project brought space travel and space research one step closer to the average American. By practicing demanding escape procedures, such as shimmying down a rope in a bulky orange pressurized suit, Glenn showed that an older man can be agile. By enduring cramped space for exercise and relating amicably with a younger, more experienced crew, he showed that an older man can adapt gracefully. He proved that even a seventy-seven-year-old could undergo an intensive month of training, prepare for 83 experiments, master knowledge of 2,600 cargo items, and learn the function of the 850 toggle switches of the *Discovery* shuttle. If he could do it, perhaps some day soon, anyone could.

ESCAPE FROM THE EARTHLY ENVIRONMENT

Walter Cronkite, the CBS evening news anchor from 1962 to 1981, discusses in a brief essay for Newsweek, *entitled "And That's the Way It Was," the impact of Glenn's first epic trip into space and how that experience makes the second trip worthwhile.*

"It's difficult to remember now how impossibly dangerous space flight seemed. The stakes couldn't have been higher, nor the risks greater: we were in a cold-war space race, we fought then, for control of the very heavens. Each of those missions—especially John Glenn's first orbital flight—was highly experimental. It was all part of the proving experience—from solo flights in the Mercury program to Apollo's lunar missions. All in one decade—an amazing feat of will, brains and bravery. The race to the moon was, I think, the quintessential story of the American Century—and I covered a lot of the others, from war to assassination to riot. Our escape from our earthly environment is what will dominate history's memory of us a half millennium from now. And that's the way it should be. Along the way, I, like so many millions of other Americans, never lost my sense of wonder or my respect for the sense of dedication at NASA. Everyone always looked up—there was a feeling that we were going to the stars. It was just a matter of money, and of how willing we were to experiment with people's lives. In the first days of the space program, reporters like me had to go back to school, to study and learn. We had to master all sorts of strange physical laws, like the fact that in space, you slow up by going faster and go faster by slowing down. . . .

I think it's great that John Glenn is going up one last time. He's a true American hero at a time when heroes are in short supply."

The space shuttle Discovery, *with John Glenn aboard, is launched from Cape Canaveral, Florida.*

"BACK TO EARTH"

Glenn's takeoff on October 29, 1998, at 2:15 P.M. was witnessed by 1,500 journalists and 250,000 spectators. Nationwide coverage of the launch mimicked that of *Friendship 7*, and even featured Walter Cronkite, the CBS anchor who had narrated the Project Mercury orbits thirty-six years before. Annie watched again, this time with her grandchildren and son, and she received an e-mail message from her husband instead of a telephone call. According to *New York Times* reporter Thomas Mallon, Annie's reaction as she watched the launch was, "John's like a cat with nine lives. [If something happens], I will always live with the idea that John went the way John would like to. That's been my way of life, I think."[112]

From 345 miles above Earth in *Discovery*, Glenn could see the United States from Florida to Lake Erie. "It's quite something," he said, "to look down on this blue planet, seeing that little film of air that surrounds it. You fly over the Mediterranean, over the Middle East—and it's so beautiful. You wonder why in the world humans can't solve all the problems they've created and left to fester over the centuries."[113]

His eight days in space, and his safe return on November 6, 1998, brought Glenn a hero's welcome. At the New York City ticker-tape parade on November 30, 1998, five hundred thousand people flocked to follow him down Broadway's "Canyon of Heroes," ushering in a week of nothing but celebrations.

Annie also enjoyed the limelight of Glenn's *Discovery* flight, although mostly for his sake. However, after a 75-year relationship with Glenn, she called for a change. Following the New York parade, she said she looked forward to the time when "John and I will just be together someplace on the road. . . . It's about time I can take him back as my own."[114]

THE RESULTS OF THE MISSION

Glenn was undeniably happy with the role he played in medical experimentation. He provided blood and urine samples, was catheterized for blood tests en route, swallowed bite-size thermometers, and wore a clumsy headset of electronic sensors. He felt that in his role of payload specialist, or onboard scientist, he had made a worthwhile scientific contribution. Besides, as Mark Alpert in *Scientific American* writes, he shared the flight that

> released and retrieved the Spartan 201 satellite, which provided striking images of the sun's corona . . . ; [tested] a platform of instruments that will be installed on the Hubble Space Telescope in 2000 . . . ; [conducted] dozens of experiments . . . in the shuttle's Spacehab laboratory, including a study to determine whether near-perfect crystals of human insulin can be grown in zero gravity.[115]

The results of Glenn's time on *Discovery* were released early in 2000. NASA scientists disclosed that he "suffered no more loss of bone mass or muscle than younger astronauts. And his heart rate, before, during and after the flight actually was slightly better than the average of 12 younger male astronauts."[116]

TWO HEROES FOR THE PRICE OF ONE

In his article "The Last Heroes: John Glenn Flies Us Back to the Age of Innocence" for Life *magazine, Richard B. Stolley discusses Glenn's own hero, his wife, Annie.*

"Great love stories are in short supply in Washington these days. This is one of them. They grew up together, their parents were good friends. The only times they were separated were when John went to war or into space. This summer, when the old fighter pilot flew himself to training sessions in Houston in his Beechcraft, Annie was beside him, checking logs and charts, his indispensable partner.

There is one thing John Glenn would like the world to know about the former Anna Margaret Castor, his wife of 55 years. 'She has more guts than people are aware of, and this doesn't have anything to do with the space program.' At a young age, Annie developed a virtually uncontrollable stutter. 'I knew her for the kind of person she was,' Glenn says, 'and it didn't bother me. But the telephone is the invention of the devil for a stutterer, and when I was away in the Marines, she wouldn't use it. She was physically unable to pick up the phone.' The Glenns lined up neighbors in case of an emergency. 'If something happened to one of the kids,' Glenn says, 'Annie could run over, bang on the door, and the neighbor would make the call.'

Annie had difficulty dealing with the public and press after John's space flight. 'A couple of times there were jokes about her,' Glenn recalls, his voice low and angry. 'That was the closest I ever came to homicide.' Then, about 20 years ago, the Glenns saw a story on TV about a program for stutterers at Hollins College in Roanoke, Virginia. Annie enrolled, and her improvement was dramatic. She decided to take her new skills on the campaign trail. 'Never given a speech in her life, but she was absolutely determined,' he recalls. 'She spoke to a women's group in Canton, and there wasn't a dry eye in the house. I can't tell you how much I admire her. She's shown a lot of courage in dealing with my life, but she has a personal courage of her own that is just outstanding.'"

The data effectively demonstrated the healthful effect of Glenn's regular exercise and good nutrition. Dr. Alfred Rossum, who participated in the cardiovascular tests on Glenn, found the returns unremarkable. He says, "Here we had in John Glenn someone who has done nothing but take care of himself for a lifetime and we get these surprising results."[117]

A MISSION AT OHIO STATE UNIVERSITY

As Glenn's fourth Senate term came to a close, he looked back on his career with pride. As a pilot, he had served his country in two wars. As an astronaut, he had been the first person to orbit Earth. And as a senator, he had cast close to ten thousand votes on measures regarding health, the environment, civil rights, education, military readiness, and the future of science. With those accomplishments behind him, Glenn felt certain that he had left a legacy to the next generation of U.S. citizens.

Glenn took that legacy one step further when, in 1999, he founded the John Glenn Institute for Public Service and Public Policy at Ohio State University in Columbus. The institute's mission is to encourage younger citizens to enter politics, and its website reports that it "is committed to enhancing public service opportunities and experiences for students as well as examining and enhancing the state of public service in America today."[118]

This philosophy is put into action through various institute activities and pro-grams. An annual survey of Americans' ideas about citizenship and research opportunities are two examples. Further, public officials are invited to visit, and a yearly Glenn National Conference addresses contemporary public issues.

When he is not traveling and enjoying his retirement, John Glenn plays an active role in the institute that bears his name and embodies his dream for the future of public service. He plans to host radio and television shows, produced at the university stations, and to make politics and public service accessible and appealing to America's youth. As Glenn told Jeffrey Kluger of *Time* shortly before his flight training for the *Discovery* mission, he worries about the future of a nation whose youngest generations see politics through jaded and apathetic eyes:

> I worry about the future when we have so many young people who feel apathetic and critical and cynical about anything having to do with politics. They don't want to touch it. And yet politics is literally the personnel system for democracy. We've got the finest democracy in the world, but it's also one of the most complicated. Not everyone needs to run for public office, but every time someone drops out of the system it means they in effect give their franchise [vote] to somebody else.[119]

Glenn hopes that America's youth will listen to the ideas of an old space traveler. If they do not, though, he will always be satisfied that he gave it his best shot.

Notes

Introduction: An American Hero

1. Charles Krauthammer, "What Happened to Destiny?" *Time*, November 9, 1998, p. 130.

Chapter 1: An All-American Boyhood

2. Quoted in Peter N. Carroll, *Famous in America: The Passion to Succeed*. New York: E. P. Dutton, 1985, p. 68.
3. John Glenn with Nick Taylor, *John Glenn: A Memoir*. New York: Bantam Books, 1999, p. 6.
4. Glenn, *John Glenn*, p. 14.
5. Glenn, *John Glenn*, p. 11.
6. Glenn, *John Glenn*, p. 18.
7. Glenn, *John Glenn*, p. 21.
8. Glenn, *John Glenn*, p. 29.
9. Quoted in Carroll, *Famous in America*, p. 69.
10. Glenn, *John Glenn*, pp. 37–38.
11. Glenn, *John Glenn*, p. 33.
12. Glenn, *John Glenn*, p. 31.
13. Glenn, *John Glenn*, p. 37.
14. Glenn, *John Glenn*, p. 39.
15. Glenn, *John Glenn*, p. 45.
16. Glenn, *John Glenn*, p. 48.
17. Glenn, *John Glenn*, p. 49.
18. Glenn, *John Glenn*, p. 51.
19. M. Scott Carpenter et al., *We Seven, by the Astronauts Themselves*. New York: Simon & Schuster, 1962, p. 35.
20. Carpenter, *We Seven, by the Astronauts Themselves*, p. 36.
21. Glenn, *John Glenn*, p. 53.

Chapter 2: A Soldier in Two Wars

22. Glenn, *John Glenn*, p. 60.
23. Glenn, *John Glenn*, p. 69.
24. Quoted in Glenn, *John Glenn*, p. 71.
25. Glenn, *John Glenn*, p. 72.
26. Glenn, *John Glenn*, p. 80.
27. Glenn, *John Glenn*, p. 92.
28. Glenn, *John Glenn*, p. 93.
29. Glenn, *John Glenn*, p. 95.
30. Glenn, *John Glenn*, p. 108.
31. Glenn, *John Glenn*, pp. 111–12.
32. Glenn, *John Glenn*, p. 115.
33. Glenn, *John Glenn*, p. 119.
34. Glenn, *John Glenn*, p. 121.
35. Philip N. Pierce and Karl Schuon, *John H. Glenn, Astronaut*. New York: Franklin Watts, 1962, p. 43.

Chapter 3: Test Pilot

36. Carroll, *Famous in America*, p. 71.
37. Quoted in Frank Van Riper, *Glenn: The Astronaut Who Would Be President*. New York, Empire Books, 1983, p. 109.
38. Quoted in Van Riper, *Glenn*, p. 111.
39. Glenn, *John Glenn*, p. 156.
40. Carroll, *Famous in America*, pp. 71–72.
41. Quoted in Van Riper, *Glenn*, p. 112.
42. Van Riper, *Glenn*, p. 113.
43. Carroll, *Famous in America*, p. 73.
44. Van Riper, *Glenn*, p. 118.
45. Vincent Canby, "Catching Up," *New York Times*, October 21, 1983, p. C5.
46. Van Riper, *Glenn*, p. 121.
47. Quoted in Van Riper, *Glenn*, p. 122.
48. Quoted in Van Riper, *Glenn*, p. 123.

Chapter 4: The First American Astronaut to Orbit Earth

49. Quoted in Glenn, *John Glenn*, pp. 193–94.
50. Glenn, *John Glenn*, p. 229.
51. Carpenter, *We Seven, by the Astronauts Themselves*, p. 195.
52. Glenn, *John Glenn*, p. 220.
53. Glenn, *John Glenn*, p. 221.

54. Glenn, *John Glenn*, p. 221.

55. Quoted in Richard B. Stolley, "The Last Heroes: John Glenn Flies Us Back to the Age of Innocence," *Life*, October 1998, p. 68.

56. Carpenter, *We Seven, by the Astronauts Themselves*, p. 384.

57. Carpenter, *We Seven, by the Astronauts Themselves*, pp. 387–88.

58. Robert B. Voas, "John Glenn's Three Orbits in *Friendship 7*," *National Geographic*, June 1962, p. 825.

59. Loudon Wainwright and Paul Mandel, "He Hit That Keyhole in the Sky," *Life*, March 1962, p. 40.

60. Glenn, *John Glenn*, p. 278.

61. Glenn, *John Glenn*, p. 281.

62. *National Geographic*, "John Glenn Receives the Society's Hubbard Medal," June 1962, p. 827.

63. Carroll, *Famous in America*, p. 85.

Chapter 5: A Hero with Other Work to Do

64. Van Riper, *Glenn*, p. 179.

65. Van Riper, *Glenn*, p. 179.

66. Carroll, *Famous in America*, p. 133.

67. Carroll, *Famous in America*, p. 134.

68. Quoted in Carroll, *Famous in America*, pp. 137–38.

69. Quoted in Howard Kohn, "How John Glenn Got Rich," *Rolling Stone*, November 24, 1981, p. 76.

70. Ralph Waldo Emerson, *Emerson: Essays and Lectures*. New York: Library of America, 1983, p. 379.

71. Van Riper, *Glenn*, pp. 225–26.

72. Glenn, *John Glenn*, p. 324.

73. Quoted in Susan Schindehette, Margery Sellinger, and Macon Morehouse, "The Final Frontier," *People*, October 26, 1998, p. 120.

74. Van Riper, *Glenn*, pp. 229–30.

75. Quoted in Van Riper, *Glenn*, p. 230.

76. Van Riper, *Glenn*, pp. 236–37.

77. Glenn, *John Glenn*, p. 327.

78. Quoted in Schindehette, Sellinger, and Morehouse, "The Final Frontier," p. 120.

79. Quoted in Richard F. Fenno Jr., *The Presidential Odyssey of John Glenn*, Washington, DC: Congressional Quarterly, 1990, p. 19.

80. Quoted in Van Riper, *Glenn*, p. 264.

81. Quoted in Carroll, *Famous in America*, p. 211.

Chapter 6: The Public Service Politician

82. Glenn, *John Glenn*, p. 337.

83. Glenn, *John Glenn*, p. 341.

84. Glenn, *John Glenn*, p. 363.

85. John Glenn, in *A Report by the Staff of the Subcommittee on Energy, Nuclear Proliferation, and Federal Services*. Washington, DC: U.S. Government Printing Office, 1980, p. vii.

86. General Accounting Office, *Actions Being Taken to Help Reduce Occupational Radiation Exposure at Commercial Nuclear Powerplants*, Washington, DC: U.S. Government Printing Office, August 24, 1982, p. i.

87. Glenn, *John Glenn*, p. 333.

88. Carroll, *Famous in America*, p. 260.

89. Quoted in Carroll, *Famous in America*, p. 261.

90. Quoted in Carroll, *Famous in America*, p. 261.

91. Quoted in Fenno, *The Presidential Odyssey of John Glenn*, p. 32.

92. Fenno, *The Presidential Odyssey of John Glenn*, p. 65.

93. Quoted in Fenno, *The Presidential Odyssey of John Glenn*, p. 65.

94. Glenn, *John Glenn*, p. 344.

95. Glenn, *John Glenn*, p. 347.

96. Van Riper, *Glenn*, p. 329.

97. Fenno, *The Presidential Odyssey of John Glenn*, pp. 67–68.

98. Tom Morganthau, Richard Manning, and

Howard Fineman, "Glenn Meets the Dream Machine," *Newsweek*, October 3, 1983, p. 37.

99. Quoted in Fenno, *The Presidential Odyssey of John Glenn*, p. 92.

100. Glenn, *John Glenn*, p. 350.

101. Fenno, *The Presidential Odyssey of John Glenn*, p. 267.

Chapter 7: Back in Orbit

102. John Glenn and John Warner, *Persian Gulf: Report to the Majority Leader, United States Senate, from Senator John Glenn and Senator John Warner on Their Trip to the Persian Gulf, May 27–June 4, 1987*. Washington, DC: U.S. Government Printing Office, 1987, p. 20.

103. Glenn, *John Glenn*, p. 355.

104. Glenn, *John Glenn*, pp. 356–57.

105. Glenn, *John Glenn*, p. 358.

106. Stolley, "The Last Heroes," p. 50.

107. Quoted in Glenn, *John Glenn*, p. 366.

108. Quoted in Glenn, *John Glenn*, p. 370.

109. Quoted in Matt Bai, "The Time Traveler," *Newsweek*, October 26, 1998, p. 33.

110. Geoffrey Cowley and Anne Underwood, "Exploring the Secrets of Age," *Newsweek*, October 26, 1998, p. 39.

111. Bai, "The Time Traveler," p. 33.

112. Quoted in Thomas Mallon, "Space Aged," *New York Times Magazine*, June 14, 1998, p. 54.

113. Quoted in William R. Newcott, "John Glenn: Man with a Mission," *National Geographic*, June 1999, p. 81.

114. Quoted in *People*, "Sky High," November 30, 1998, p. 65.

115. Mark Alpert, "John Glenn's Excellent Adventure," *Scientific American*, January 1999, p. 31.

116. Associated Press, "Glenn Handled Rigors of Space Well, Scientists Report," *Missoulian*, January 29, 2000, p. A3.

117. Quoted in Associated Press, "Glenn Handled Rigors of Space Well, Scientists Report," p. A3.

118. John Glenn Institute for Public Service and Public Policy, "Key Program Areas of the John Glenn Institute." www.osu.edu/units/ucomm/Glenn/Offerings.htm.

119. Quoted in Jeffrey Kluger, "The Soul of a Senator," *Time*, August 17, 1998, p. 50.

For Further Reading

Books

David S. Akens, *John Glenn, First American in Orbit*. Huntsville, AL: Strode, 1969. Concentrates mainly on the Mercury Project but also has brief coverage of Glenn after retirement from the marines. Many full-page illustrations are included.

Peter A. Campbell, *Launch Day*. Brookfield, CT: Millbrook, 1995. Describes preparation, launch, and return of the *Atlantis* space shuttle at Cape Kennedy Space Center; easy reading.

Paul Clark, *Famous Names in Space Exploration*. East Sussex, England: Wayland, 1978. Provides one to three pages each on space explorers from Jules Verne to Carl Sagan and Gerard O'Neill.

Michael D. Cole, *"Friendship 7": First American in Orbit*. Hillside, NJ: Enslow, 1995. An appealing portrait of an American hero and astronaut, covering through 1991. This illustrated book is easy reading.

———, *John Glenn, Astronaut and Senator*. Hillside, NJ: Enslow, 1993. This illustrated book emphasizes astronomy and politics.

Chris Crocker, *Great American Astronauts*. New York: Franklin Watts, 1988. Fifteen chapters on topics from individual astronauts to Projects Mercury and Apollo and projections for the future.

Robert White Hill, *What Colonel Glenn Did All Day*. New York: Franklin Watts, 1962. Provides detailed information on Glenn's work with Project Mercury.

Barbara Kramer, *John Glenn: A Space Biography*. Springfield, NJ: Enslow, 1998. This fairly technical book, intended for intermediate readers, ends with Glenn's resignation from the Senate.

Stephanie Maze, *I Want to Be an Astronaut*. San Diego: Harcourt Brace, 1997. Describes what it is like to be an astronaut, some of the ways to prepare for this career, and various jobs of astronauts.

Sally Ride and Susan Okie, *To Space and Back*. New York: Lothrop & Shepard, 1986. Astronaut Sally Ride gives a day-by-day description of her work on the space shuttle *Discovery*. Contains many great photos.

James A. Seevers, *Space*. Milwaukee: Raintree, 1978. An easy-to-read overview of space exploration with comments on the metric system.

Paul Westman, *John Glenn: Around the World in Ninety Minutes*. Minneapolis:

Dillon, 1979. Concentrates on Glenn's boyhood and on his Earth orbit. Very easy reading and illustrated.

Periodicals

Editors of Aviation Week, *Aviation Week and Space Technology*, December 31, 1990. Name the year and you will find historical features on milestones of space exploration, with great illustrations of people and technology.

U.S. News & World Report, "New Adventures in Space," July 16, 1979. A retrospect on the space program with emphasis on the Apollo mission to the Moon.

Works Consulted

Books

M. Scott Carpenter et al., *We Seven, by the Astronauts Themsleves*. New York: Simon & Schuster, 1962. Includes technology, personal details, and memories about Project Mercury from the point of view of each of the seven astronauts.

Peter N. Carroll, *Famous in America: The Passion to Succeed*. New York: E. P. Dutton, 1985. A four-part biography coordinated with biographies of three other famous people: George Wallace, Jane Fonda, and Phyllis Schlafly. Contains many personal details and an analysis of success.

Ralph Waldo Emerson, *Emerson: Essays and Lectures*. New York: Library of America, 1983. Collected works of the nineteenth-century American essayist.

Richard F. Fenno Jr., *The Presidential Odyssey of John Glenn*. Washington, DC: Congressional Quarterly, 1990. Short treatment of Glenn's prepolitical career followed by documentation on and analysis of his presidential campaign.

The First Man in Space: The Record of Yuri Gagarin's First Venture into Cosmic Space, a Collection of Translations from Soviet Press Reports. New York: Cross-Currents, 1961. A documentary account of Russia's space hero and space achievements told by Soviet newswriters. Called "a memento of the spaceship *Vostok*'s voyage, the articles report, interpret, and give technical and scientific information. Also includes an interview and brief biography of Gagarin.

John Glenn with Nick Taylor, *John Glenn: A Memoir*. New York: Bantam Books, 1999. Glenn's autobiographical commentary on his life and times with many personal insights.

John Glenn, ed., *Letters to John Glenn, with Comments by J. H. Glenn, Jr.* Washington, DC: World Book Encyclopedia Science Service, 1964. Selected letters received by Glenn after his orbit of Earth.

William J. Koenig, *Americans at War: From the Colonial Wars to Vietnam*. London: Bison Books, 1980. Lucid twenty-page chapters explain and chronicle twelve wars. Contemporary art and photo illustrations are included.

Philip N. Pierce and Karl Schuon, *John H. Glenn, Astronaut*. New York: Franklin Watts, 1962. This young adult biography has many exciting conversations with Glenn about preparing for spaceflight and his time in the *Friendship 7* module.

Values Americans Live By. New York: New York Times Company/Grolier Education Corporation, 1978. Reprints from the *New York Times*.

Frank Van Riper, *Glenn: The Astronaut Who Would be President.* New York: Empire Books, 1983. An analytical treatment of Glenn's aspirations to the presidency, considering his patterns of thought and behavior from childhood through his presidential campaign.

Tom Wolfe, *The Right Stuff.* New York: Farrar, Straus, & Giroux, 1979. A riveting, descriptive, and personalized report on every aspect of the men and the program that took the United States into the space age.

Pamphlets and Documents

John Glenn and John Warner, *Persian Gulf: Report to the Majority Leader, United States Senate, from Senator John Glenn and Senator John Warner on Their Trip to the Persian Gulf, May 27–June 4, 1987.* Washington, DC: U.S. Government Printing Office, 1987.

John Glenn, *Rethinking Defense and Conventional Forces.* Washington, DC: Center for National Policy, 1983.

———, *U.S. Troop Withdrawal from the Republic of Korea, an Update, 1979: A Report to the Committee on Foreign Relations, United States Senate.* Washington, DC: U.S. Government Printing Office, 1979.

Manned Spacecraft Center, *Results of the First U.S. Manned Orbital Space Flight,* *February 20, 1962.* Washington, DC: U.S. Government Printing Office, 1962.

Senate Select Committee on Ethics, *Preliminary Inquiry into Allegations Regarding Senators Cranston, DeConcini, Glenn, McCain, and Riegle, and Lincoln Savings and Loan: Open Session Hearings before the Select Committee on Ethics,* 101st Cong., 2nd sess., 1991.

Periodicals

Mark Alpert, "John Glenn's Excellent Adventure," *Scientific American,* January 1999.

David Ansen with Katrine Ames, "A Movie with All the Right Stuff," *Newsweek,* October 3, 1983.

Associated Press, "John Glenn Handled Rigors of Space Well, Scientists Report," *Missoulian,* January 29, 2000.

Matt Bai, "The Time Traveler," *Newsweek,* October 26, 1998.

———, "The Ultimate Last Hurrah," *Newsweek,* January 26, 1998.

———, "Zero-G and I Feel Fine," *Newsweek,* November 9, 1998.

Amy Borrus, "John Glenn, Donorgate Pit Bull," *Business Week,* July 21, 1997.

Vincent Canby, "Catching Up," *New York Times,* October 21, 1983.

Geoffrey Cowley and Anne Underwood, "Exploring the Secrets of Age," *Newsweek,* October 26, 1998.

Allison Frazier, "They Gave Us Space," *To the Stars*, January/February, 2000.

Robert R. Gilruth, "The Making of an Astronaut," *National Geographic*, June 1962.

John Glenn, "If You're Shook Up, You Shouldn't Be There," *Life*, March 9, 1962.

Paula Goldman, "This Time Out, He Had the Wrong Stuff," *Newsweek*, November/December 1984.

Dora Jean Hamblin, "Applause, Tears, and Laughter and the Emotions of a Long-Ago Fourth of July," *Life*,.

Jeffrey Kluger, "The Right Stuff, Thirty-Six Years Later," *Time*, January 26, 1998.

———, "The Soul of a Senator," *Time*, August 17, 1998.

———, "Victory Lap," *Time*, November 9, 1998.

Howard Kohn, "How John Glenn Got Rich," *Rolling Stone*, November 24, 1981.

Charles Krauthammer, "What Happened to Destiny?" *Time*, November 9, 1998.

Thomas Mallon, "Space Aged," *New York Times Magazine*, June 14, 1998.

Tom Morganthau with Richard Manning and Howard Fineman, "Glenn: Into the Trenches," *Newsweek*, November 28, 1983.

———"Glenn Meets the Dream Machine," *Newsweek*, October 3, 1983.

National Geographic. "John Glenn Receives the Society's Hubbard Medal," June 1962.

William R. Newcott, "John Glenn: Man with a Mission," *National Geographic*, June 1999.

Newsweek, "Glenn: A Mission in Fence-Mending," September 26, 1983.

People, "John Glenn: The Sky Proved No Limit," December 28, 1998–January 4, 1999.

———, "Sky High," November 30, 1998.

Susan Schindlhette, Margery Sellinger, and Macon Morehouse, "The Final Frontier," *People,* October 26, 1998.

Joseph P. Shapiro, "John Glenn's Mixed Message on Aging," *U.S. News & World Report*, November 16, 1998.

Richard B. Stolley, "The Last Heroes: John Glenn Flies Us Back to the Age of Innocence," *Life*, 1998.

Dick Thompson, "Back to the Future," *Time*, August 17, 1998.

Robert B. Voas, "John Glenn's Three Orbits in *Friendship 7*," *National Geographic*, June 1962.

Loudon Wainwright and Paul Mandel, "He Hit That Keyhole in the Sky," *Life*, March 1962.

Internet Sources

William J. Clinton, "Statement on the Non-Proliferation of Nuclear Weapons Treaty," Weekly Compilation of Presidential Documents, March 13, 2000. http://web5.infotrac.../purl=rc.

John Glenn Institute for Public Service and Public Policy, "Key Program Areas and Offerings of the John Glenn Institute. www.osu.edu/units/ucomm/Glenn /Offerings.htm.

Renee Juhans and Peter Cleary, "Glenn to Discuss Space Flight, Aging Stud-ies May 25," *NASA News*, May 19, 1990. http://spaceflight.nasa.gov/ spacenews/releases/N99-30.html.

NASA Website, www.nasa.gov.

Office of Space Flight, "John Glenn, First American in Orbit," 1998. www.hq.nasa.gov.osf/1998/yearinrev/ 98table3.html.

Index

Picture Credits

Cover photo: NASA/CNP/Archive Photos

© Aero Graphics, Inc./Corbis, 86

© AFP/Corbis, 101

APA/Archive Photos, 42

Archive Photos, 41, 62, 63, 90

© Bettmann/Corbis, 13, 32, 39, 45, 51, 54 (right), 68, 83

ClassMates.com Yearbook Archives, 17

CNP/Archive Photos, 71

© Corbis, 33, 93

© Owen Franken/Corbis, 76

Library of Congress, 49

© Museum of Flight/Corbis, 25

NASA, 54 (left), 58, 99

National Archives, 28

Popperfoto/Archive Photos, 21, 69

© Roger Ressmeyer/Corbis, 36, 46, 97

Reuters/Ralph Alswang/Archive Photos, 94

Sachs/CNP/Archive Photos, 95

Reuters/Dominique Dudouble/Archive Photos, 80

About the Author

Rafael Tilton is an educator, editor, and writer who has written five other books for young people. Tilton's interest in science, sparked by high school courses in physics and chemistry, has continued through a lifelong program of scientific reading. Coming from a family that never shied away from political discussion, Tilton is sympathetic to many of the issues that engaged Senator John Glenn.